THE  BOOK OF THE
F-16
FIGHTING FALCON

TIM SENIOR

KEY
BOOKS

Below: These F-16Cs form part of the 57th FW at Nellis AFB, Nevada and serve in the role of adversary training aircraft, and are painted to represent various aircraft from the Soviet era such as the Sukhoi Su-27 Flanker as illustrated here. (Rick Llinares)

Key Books Ltd
PO Box 100, Stamford, Lincolnshire PE9 1XQ
United Kingdom

Telephone: +44 (0) 1780 755131
E-mail: keybooks@keypublishing.com

First published in Great Britain by Key Books Ltd in 2002

ISBN 0-946219-60-5

British Library Cataloguing in Publication Data:
A catalogue record for this book is available from the British Library

Designed by DAG Publications Ltd
Printed in Spain by Book Print

The editor wishes to point out that the material supplied by Shlomo Aloni was limited to photographs passed by the Israeli censor only, and that he played no part whatsoever in writing the captions in this book, which have been compiled from openly available material.

This Belgian AF F-16A was painted to represent a falcon, to celebrate the 20th anniversary of the F-16 entering service with the Belgian forces and comes complete with its own pair of talons on the underside of the fuselage. (KEY – Steve Fletcher)

CONTENTS

① INTRODUCTION

Lockheed Martin's F-16 Fighting Falcon has been in service with the United States Air Force (USAF) and with the air forces of Belgium, Denmark, Norway and the Netherlands for over 20 years. In January 1981, the 388th Tactical Fighter Wing (TFW) at Hill Air Force Base (AFB), Utah, became the USAF's first operational F-16 unit and still flies the aircraft today. Now established as one of the world's most versatile fighter aircraft, the F-16 serves with all these countries – and with many other nations – and will continue to do so for at least another 20 years. Remarkably, it is also still in production.

Though similar in appearance to the aircraft that first flew during the early 1970s, current production versions of the Fighting Falcon are true multi-role fighters compared to the aircraft which emerged as the winner of the 1972 Lightweight Fighter (LWF) competition. The early model F-16s were designed as 'no frills', lightweight and agile fighter aircraft to complement a new larger aircraft then in the design phase, which later became the McDonnell Douglas F-15 Eagle. Constant improvements have ensured that the F-16 remains at the forefront of technology.

Although conceived as a lightweight air superiority day fighter, it has proved to be an excellent aircraft in the air-to-ground role. The USAF decided to utilise the aircraft in this role, despite the fact that the F-16 had at first failed to interest senior USAF officers and planners who feared that the lightweight fighter would jeopardise plans to purchase the heavier, costlier, though significantly more capable, F-15. Eventually, the USAF ordered the aircraft on January 13, 1975. On June 7 the same year, the governments of Belgium, Denmark, the Netherlands and Norway announced that they had also selected the F-16. These four countries had rejected the Northrop YF-17 and a private venture version of this, the Northrop P-530 Cobra. The Anglo-French Sepecat Jaguar was also eliminated early in the competition. This left two other main contenders – the Dassault Mirage F1 and the Saab Viggen, and these, too, were rejected.

The F-16 has since overtaken the Eagle as the most widely-used aircraft in the current USAF inventory, notching up more than twice as many orders from the USAF as the twin-engined Eagle. The USAF went on to order over 2,300 of the four main production versions of the F-16, and almost all of these had been delivered by the beginning of 2001. All the production versions of the F-16s – with the exception of both the prototypes and the Full-Scale-Development (FSD) aircraft – had a block number allocated to them while they were under construction.

The block number system implemented by General Dynamics is still used by Lockheed Martin, and basically signifies an aircraft built to a certain standard – thus the first F-16A and B aircraft from early production orders were built to Block 1 standard. Upon completion of these orders, a gap was introduced, the next batch of aircraft being built to Block 5 standard. The remaining batches were also built with this gap, meaning that the next batch to be built was Block 10, and the final Block number allocated for production of the A and B model aircraft was Block 15. The vacant Block 20 slot was used at a much later date.

F-16C and D model production started with Block number 25, though a change in the system began with the introduction of the Block 30 series aircraft as there was a choice of two different powerplants, from Pratt & Whitney (Block 32) and General Electric (Block 30). Subsequent Blocks have a gap of ten between them: consequently the next batches produced became the Block 40/42, followed by the current production Block 50/52, with the new Block 60 series to come. However, some smaller changes have been introduced to aircraft on the production line. Referred to as 'miniblocks', these are denoted by letters after the block number.

The first production F-16A made its maiden flight on August 7, 1979, and first deliveries of production aircraft were made to the 388 TFW at Hill AFB, Utah, on November 12, 1980. When the F-16 entered service, it initially replaced the early models of the McDonnell Douglas F-4 Phantom II in regular USAF service, enabling

Above: An early photograph of the General Dynamics production line at Fort Worth, Texas. This view gives some idea of the scale of work involved in the production of the F-16. In the distance, some of the smaller sections are awaiting final assembly. The nearest aircraft is part of the first batch of F-16s for the USAF: this aircraft became 78-0007 and served until it was retired to AMARC at Davis-Monthan AFB, Arizona, in September 1994. (General Dynamics)

Bottom: An F-16C from the 416th Flight Test Squadron, based at Edwards Air Force Base, California, launches an AIM-120 AMRAAM at one of the US Navy's test ranges over the Pacific Ocean. (USAF/Tom Reynolds)

Top: Two early production Block 5 F-16As escort one of the most successful American fighter aircraft of the Second World War – the North American P-51 Mustang. Both are being flown by company test pilots and had not entered service at the time this photograph was taken. (Robert F Dorr collection)

Centre: The 1,000th F-16 produced was a Block 15, and was photographed flying over the Fort Worth production facility shortly after being handed over to the USAF. Entering service as F-16A 82-0926, it was delivered to the 388th TFW in July 1983. It subsequently underwent conversion to F-16 ADF standard and was still serving with the 178th FS, North Dakota ANG, in 2001. (Robert F Dorr collection)

Bottom: On April 28, 2000, Lockheed Martin passed another production milestone with the hand-over to the Egyptian AF of the 4,000th F-16. This F-16C was part of the fifth batch ordered by Egypt under the Peace Vector programme. (Lockheed Martin)

units converting to pass their Phantoms on to the Air Force Reserve (AFRes) and the Air National Guard (ANG). This made it possible to retire older fighters such as the McDonnell F-101 Voodoo, and North American F-100 Super Sabre, which, due to their designations, were referred to as 'the century series'. Most of the latter would eventually fall to air-to-air missiles fired from F-16s taking part in competitions and missile trials flown from Eglin AFB and Tyndall AFB, in Florida.

As the USAF introduced newer blocks of F-16Cs and Ds into service during the early 1990s, older A and B models flown by the ANG were retired and flown to the Aerospace Maintenance and Regeneration Centre (AMARC) at Davis-Monthan AFB, Arizona, for storage. Several new customers, including Italy and Jordan, have acquired these surplus USAF aircraft, and existing customers, such as Portugal and Thailand, have also bought aircraft stored at AMARC to bolster their fleets. The prospective customer has the opportunity to choose any one of a number of the unlimited aircraft systems upgrades currently available, ensuring these F-16s a second life well into the 21st century. The US Navy, which originally acquired 26 F/TF-16Ns for aggressor training, is expected to receive part of an embargoed batch of aircraft originally destined for the Pakistan Air Force. The remaining aircraft from this batch are slated for use by the USAF for test duties. The F-16 has also provided the basis for the development of the Mitsubishi F-2, which is currently entering service with the Japanese Air Self Defence Force (JASDF).

Despite General Dynamic's 1993 merger with Lockheed and their subsequent acquisition of Martin Marietta to form Lockheed Martin, the future looks bright for the F-16 family. By August 31, 2001, total production orders for all versions of the F-16 family numbered just over 4,337, with over 300 aircraft still to be built. Licensed production in Belgium and the Netherlands ceased years ago, though plans exist for an additional production run in Turkey (at the time of writing funding for this was withheld due to various financial difficulties). Construction of a fourth batch of 20 aircraft for the Singapore Air Force was under way during early 2001, while deliveries of the sixth batch of 24 Block 40s to the Egyptian AF commenced in June 2001. Licence production of Block 52 is also about to restart in Korea, where an additional 20 aircraft are on order. Orders from new customers include Chile, which confirmed an initial order for ten Block 50s during the early part of 2001. Details were released on October 4, 2001, of the sale to Oman of 12 Block 50/52 F-16C/Ds together with associated weapons and support equipment. Additional orders could follow between 2005 and 2008 as the Omani Air Force looks to replace its Jaguar fleet. The Greek Air Force placed an order for 50 of the Block 50+ variant in 1999, and the United Arab Emirates has become the launch customer for the new Block 60 model F-16. With new advanced avionics and upgraded engines and radar, this version has already aroused interest among other existing users, and will almost certainly add to the final production total.

With both the Block 50 and 52 family and the newer Block 60, this will no doubt keep the production lines at Fort Worth running for the next ten years at least, and possibly longer – securing work until the Joint Strike Fighter (JSF) goes into full production at the Texas plant.

Above: One of the best-known units within the USAF is the aerial demonstration team, The Thunderbirds. The unit usually has a complement of seven F-16Cs and two F-16Ds. The display is flown with six aircraft: the remainder are used as spares in case one aircraft goes unserviceable. (USAF)

Left: All five of the original customers are represented in this formation of F-16As. From the top: an aircraft from 311 Squadron based at Volkel in the Netherlands; one from the USAFE 10th TFS, based at the former Hahn AFB, in Germany, which closed in 1992. Next to the Belgian aircraft from 23 Squadron at Kleine Brogel is an unidentified Royal Danish AF aircraft; in the foreground is a Norwegian AF F-16 based at Bodø. (Robert F Dorr collection)

Left: Although Precision Guided Munitions, such as this 2,000lb Mk 84 GBU-24 Paveway III, have greater accuracy and more destructive power then ever before, the emphasis during future military campaigns will be on limiting the risks to the pilot and avoiding collateral damage. As a result, various modifications and enhancements have been made to these and other 'smart' weapons. (Raytheon)

Right: The F-16 has been a very successful fighter aircraft, since its first flight in 1974. Over 4,000 aircraft have been built, over 20 countries have purchased them, and it has taken part in many combat operations around the world. The aircraft is scheduled to serve until at least 2020 and possibly longer as new upgrades and weapons systems become available. (USAF)

Below: F-16s operate in some of the harshest environments around the world, from the freezing cold of Norway to the heat of Thailand. (KEY Archive)

Below right: USAF F-16s serve with both the Air National Guard, and Air Force Reserve Command at various locations throughout the USA, and are called up to join the regular Air Force units during national emergencies. (Lockheed Martin)

Bottom: F-16A 666 from 334 Skvadron has undergone conversion to F-16AM, and is pictured over Greenland in transit to the USA for various exercises in July 2000. (Robin Polderman)

PROTOTYPES AND DEVELOPMENTS

Two prototype YF-16s were built, neither carrying weapons or radar, which made them lighter. With the centre of gravity further forward, the two prototypes also had greater manoeuvrability and both had analogue flight controls with no computer software. The first of this pair was delivered to Edwards AFB, California, for flight testing inside a Lockheed C-5 Galaxy on January 8, 1974. Its first flight on January 20, 1974, was unplanned – during high-speed taxying trials, pilot Phil Oestricher encountered a rolling divergent oscillation. This caused the aircraft to roll from side to side and scrape the dummy AIM-9 and the right stabiliser on the runway, causing some sparks. Oestricher decided it was safer to fly out of the situation, and went on to complete an uneventful, if somewhat, unscheduled, six-minute flight. The first official planned flight – on February 2 – lasted 90 minutes. The first prototype reached Mach 1 .0 for the first time on February 5 and Mach 2.0 on March 11.

The second prototype flew for the first time on May 9 with Neil Anderson at the controls. This aircraft had been scheduled to make an appearance at the 1975 Paris Air Show but was slightly damaged when it ran off the runway and skidded along on its belly at Carswell AFB, the site of General Dynamics' Fort Worth factory. The first prototype took its place in Paris, and also undertook a tour of those European countries which had already ordered the aircraft.

During the fly-off competition against the YF-17, the two YF-16s flew a total of 330 missions and 417 flight hours, reaching speeds above Mach 2.0 and altitudes above 60,000ft (18,288m), performing manoeuvres up to 9g. The two aircraft also flew in combat trials against other USAF aircraft then in service, and used the opportunity to give as many pilots as possible the chance to fly the aircraft. At the end of their flying careers, the second prototype moved to the Rome Air Development Centre in New York, to be used in non-flying electronic test duties. The first aircraft was converted into the YF-16 Control

Right: The first prototype YF-16, seen in the early days of flight trials when it was painted in this attractive colour scheme. Five companies originally submitted designs for the lightweight fighter (LWF) programme – Boeing, General Dynamics, Lockheed, LTV Aerospace and Northrop. However, only GD and Northrop won the competition to build two prototypes for the LWF programme. The idea of two companies building a prototype and competing for the same order was nothing new – all major aircraft purchased by the United States Army Air Corps (USAAC), the predecessor of the USAF, were purchased in this way. (Robert F Dorr Collection)

Below: The second prototype initially received this blue and white colour scheme, originally intended to make the aircraft less visible in the sky. However, it was not very successful and was soon replaced by an air defence grey colour scheme. (KEY Archive)

Configured Vehicle (CCV); modifications consisting of a pair of vertical canards mounted beneath the air intake in a splayed inverted V-configuration, and flight controls permitting the use of wing trailing-edge flaperons in combination with the all-moving stabilator. These modifications began on the aircraft's return from its European trip, and it made its first flight in this configuration on March 16, 1976. All went well until its 29th flight, on June 24, when it suffered an engine failure while landing. Although seriously damaged, it was deemed to be repairable, and with repairs complete, the programme continued until July 31, 1977. A total of 87 sorties and 125 flying hours were logged by the aircraft, and these tests paved the way for the more radical AFTI/F-16, which will be described later.

In addition to the two prototypes, General Dynamics built eight Full-Scale Development (FSD) aircraft: six were single-seaters and the other two were two-seaters. Most of these airframes have led interesting lives, and several are currently on the NASA inventory, although they are inactive at the time of writing. The first versions of the radar destined to equip the production versions of the F-16 were installed in the FSD aircraft, the deeper nose being able to accommodate this. Other improved features included the enlarged ventral fins, a redesigned single-piece nosewheel door, and a larger tailplane. The first FSD aircraft, an F-16A, flew for the first time on December 8, 1976, and the first two-seater F-16B followed on August 8, 1977.

Some of the FSD airframes have been involved in various trials. The F-16/J-79 was brought about by President Jimmy Carter's arms transfer policy, which meant that

Top left: The first Full-Scale Development (FSD) aircraft was 75-0745, seen taking off for its first flight on December 8, 1976. Under the cockpit it carries the flags of the first five customers. (Robert F Dorr collection)

Above left: The first prototype YF-16 72-01567 is now preserved at the Virginia Air and Space Museum, Hampton, Virginia. The aircraft served part of its retirement as the trials airframe for studies into a potential escape system, similar to that used on earlier General Dynamic's aircraft, such as the B-58 and the F-111. This involved cutting the fuselage skin around the cockpit area and then installing the trial escape system. However, the trial was abandoned, and after several years in storage at Wright Patterson AFB, the aircraft was restored to the original prototype configuration. (KEY – Dave Willis)

Left: Two of the original single-seat F-16 FSD aircraft were converted to F-16XL configuration. The first aircraft to undergo conversion, 75-0749, is seen on an early test flight. The most obvious change is the cranked-arrow wing, developed in conjunction with NASA aerodynamics specialists. (KEY Archive)

Bottom left: Although the F-16XL could carry an impressive weapons load, it still lost out to the Boeing F-15E Strike Eagle. This was mainly due to the latter being cheaper to develop, and the aircraft was almost the same as a standard F-15C. Both F-16XLs were initially put into storage until 1989, when they were reactivated for experimental work with NASA. The aircraft joined NASA for various supersonic laminar airflow research trials at the Dryden Flight Research Center, California. Once NASA started using 75-0749 for trials, it was allocated a new serial, 849, and flew in this grey colour scheme until it was replaced by a smart black one. The first phase of laminar wing modifications can clearly be seen on 849 as it flies over the Californian desert. (Robert F Dorr collection)

some US allies were only able to receive a version of the F-16 which was less advanced than the one operated by the USAF. Although this policy did not last for long, it resulted in the simpler F-16/J-79. The aircraft used for the trials was the final FSD aircraft, F-16B 75-0752, which was bailed back to the manufacturer and fitted with a General Electric J79-GE-119 turbojet.

However, as this engine was 18in (46cm) longer than the P&W F100 engine, the rear fuselage had to be extended aft of the stabilator pivot point. Other necessary changes included a larger intake splitter plate and other changes to the intake which extended further than on any other F-16. Another disadvantage was the need to fit a 2,000lb (907kg) steel shield around most of the engine to provide heat protection; a feature not needed on turbo-fan-powered aircraft. The aircraft made its first flight on October 29, 1980. Most of the air arms expressing an interest in the F-16 – including Austria, Jordan, Malaysia, Nigeria, Singapore, Taiwan, Thailand and Venezuela – were briefed on this aircraft. The result was not entirely surprising – most preferred to purchase the full specification PW-engined A and B model. Five of these countries eventually acquired the aircraft after President Carter relaxed his policy in 1980. The election of Ronald Reagan, whose government decided that export customers would get an aircraft to the same standards as USAF aircraft, finally saw the project shelved.

The first FSD aircraft, 75-0745, had a General Electric YJ101 engine installed, and this became known as the F-16/101: the airframe made its first flight in this configuration on December 19, 1980. The YJ101 trials came about after it appeared that General Electric would lose out to Pratt & Whitney, even if the F-16/J-79 combination did sell. Despite the fact that the YJ-101, which had been installed on the YF-17 prototypes, had performed well, General Electric still wanted to demonstrate that the much-improved version, the Derivative Fighter Engine (DFE), performed better. Apart from a number of easily fixed snags, the DFE did well during the trials, though the F100 suffered a number of 'teething' problems. However, the programme ended in July 1981 without the engine being chosen for early production F-16A or B models, though it did reappear much later as the F110 engine used to power the model F-16C and D Block 30s. Having been unsuccessfully used in the F-16/J-79 programme, the eighth FSD airframe had a P&W engine refitted and was

Top Left: The single-seat F-16XL has taken part in trials with one of the NASA Lockheed SR-71s to investigate sonic booms for NASA's High Speed Research Program. During these tests, the F-16XL probed the shock waves created by the SR-71, recording their shape and intensity. Data from these trials could be used in the development of future high-speed aircraft. (NASA)

Centre left: Further aerodynamic research into laminar flow took place at Dryden with the second F-16XL proto-type. The most obvious feature here is the longer extension to the cranked wing. NASA allocated the new serial 848 to the aircraft. (NASA)

Left: The final FSD aircraft 75-0750 became the Advanced Fighter Technology Integration (AFTI) F-16, which is shown undergoing early modifications to its avionics at Fort Worth, Texas. The aircraft had not had Forward Looking Infra-Red (FLIR) fitted to the left wing root when this photograph was taken. (KEY Archive)

Top: The same aircraft seen in flight over southern California in October 1992. It now carries the AFTI/CAS titles and has lost the canards under the intake, though it has gained several FLIR sensors on the wing roots and in front of the cockpit. In 1994, it was used for Suppression of Enemy Air Defence (SEAD) trials, in which it fired an AGM-88 HARM. (NASA)

Below: Three different engines power the aircraft in this photo. The second FSD F-16B has the lengthened jetpipe and enlarged intake added for trials with the GE J79 engine. This engine was well known for its use in both the F-4 Phantom and the F-104 Starfighter. The first FSD F-16A flew trials with the GE F101 (which eventually became the F110), while the Block 5 F-16A at the rear of the formation is powered by the then-standard P&W F100 engine. (Robert F Dorr collection)

Bottom: Following the trials for the F-16/79, the final FSD aircraft was used for trials and became the F-16B-2. The aircraft had a P&W F100 engine refitted, and flew evaluation sorties with various FLIR and other sensors. (Lockheed Martin)

painted in the European One two-tone green colour scheme. It became a private venture trials aircraft, and was used to test various close air support and night/bad weather attack systems, some of which are in service with the later model F-16s flying today.

The two F-16XL are the most heavily-modified aircraft, and consequently the most easily identifiable of the entire F-16 family, due to the fact that they were converted to what is known as the 'cranked delta-wing' F-16. Two aircraft were converted to this configuration, the first being the fifth single-seat FSD aircraft (75-0749), which became XL-1 and made its first flight on July 15, 1982, with a standard P&W F100 engine. The second F-16 converted to an F-16XL was the third single-seat FSD airframe 75-0747 aircraft, though due to a landing accident, General Dynamics took the opportunity of rebuilding this into a two-seat F-16XL, which became XL-2. This was fitted with a General Electric F110 engine, derived from the engine that had been tried in the F-16/101. The conversion included an extended fuselage with two plugs inserted, one immediately in front of the forward fuel cell, which lengthened the fuselage but not the intake underneath. A second plug was added slightly aft of the mainwheel well rear bulkhead. The ventral fins found on all the other aircraft in the family were deleted, and the brake chute common to several export customers was added. During the early 1980s, the USAF was looking to replace its General Dynamics F-111s, and the F-16XL was entered into a fly-off contest with the only other contender, this being the McDonnell Douglas F-15E Strike Eagle. During the competition, the F-16XL gained the designations F-16E for the single-seat aircraft and F-16F for the two-seater.

However, on a cost projections basis, the F-15E was eventually selected. Both aircraft were then returned to storage at Fort Worth, XL-1 having completed 437 flights and XL-2 361, making a grand total of 940 flying hours. Both XL airframes gained a reprieve in 1989 when the National Air and Space Administration (NASA) signed a leasing deal to operate the two aircraft on airflow and other aerodynamic trials at supersonic speeds. Both are currently in storage at the NASA Dryden facility co-located at Edwards AFB.

The final single-seat FSD aircraft, 75-0750, has led an interesting life. Having spent its early years as the sixth F-16A FSD aircraft, it was converted into what is now known as the NF-16 Advanced Fighter Technology Integration (AFTI). Its most prominent features are the canards attached to the intake, similar to those on the earlier F-16CCV. It also had an enlarged dorsal spine for additional avionics, which is now standard fit on Israeli and Singaporean aircraft.

Over the years the aircraft gained many features from other later model F-16s, including a Block 15 standard tail section, Block 25 wings, and avionics from Block 40 standard aircraft. The AFTI NF-16 first flew in this configuration on July 10, 1982, and has since undergone substantial modifications to enable it to carry out a number of tasks. These modifications have been split into various phases, and it has been returned to the manufacturers several times for further systems upgrades. However, the AFTI has finally earned its retirement and in January 2001 it was flown to the USAF museum at Wright Patterson AFB, Ohio.

F-16A AND F-16B

Early production Block 1 F-16s differed slightly from the prototypes and pre-production aircraft in that they had a slightly larger wing and increased fuel capacity. They were also easily recognisable by the black radome, though this caused pilots to complain that it made the aircraft stick out like a sore thumb during air-to-air combat training. Other differences included a longer and deeper nose for the production standard radar, and a prominent blade aerial on the intake lip.

Sales to four NATO partners – Belgium, Denmark, the Netherlands and Norway – provided an early boost for the new aircraft. All four air forces initially required a replacement for their Lockheed F-104 Starfighters, and Denmark also needed to replace its North American F-100 Super Sabres. Later batches of aircraft replaced the Dassault Mirage V in Belgium and the Northrop F-5A/B in Norway, as well as the licence-built Canadair NF-5A/Bs in the Netherlands in the late 1980s. Aircraft started to roll off the two European production lines in mid-1979. The first of these was at Gosselies in Belgium, where Societe Anonyme Belge de Constructions Aéronautiques (SABCA) started building aircraft for the Belgian and Danish Air Forces, and the second was set up by Fokker at its Schiphol factory in the Netherlands to produce both Dutch and Norwegian aircraft. Initial orders from the four countries were for a total of 348 airframes – 116 from Belgium, 58 from Denmark, 102 from the Netherlands and 72 from Norway. All these aircraft were identical with the exception of those destined for Norway, which were equipped with a lengthened tail parachute fairing and a searchlight in the nose section for interception duties. Norway also uses its F-16s in the anti-shipping role, carrying the Penguin anti-ship missile.

These initial orders were soon followed by top-up orders, raising the figures to 160 for Belgium, and 70 for Denmark. The Norwegian government only opted for a further two airframes, while the Dutch eventually received

a total of 213. The first Belgian machine, FB-01, made its maiden flight from the Gosselies plant on December 11, 1978, and was delivered to the Air Force on January 26, 1979. The first Dutch aircraft, J-259, flew for the first time on May 3, 1979, although the first to be delivered was F-16A J-212. The first Danish aircraft (F-16B ET-204) was handed over on January 18, 1980, and Norway's first aircraft (also an F-16B) followed on January 15, 1980. Iran almost became the first non-European export customer for the Fort Worth production line; the Shah of Iran's government signed a letter of intent on October 27, 1976. A planned initial purchase of 160 aircraft was announced under the programme named 'Peace Zebra', with a possible eventual total of 300. However, the Islamic revolution soon put paid to these plans. Instead, Israel became the first real export customer in 1978 when it announced a decision to purchase 75 F-16s.

The first F-16Bs were delivered to Hill AFB, Utah, at the end of January 1980 for crew training. In the USA, several

Below: Four European Participating Air Force (EPAF) customers are illustrated in this early publicity photograph. The first production two-seaters for Denmark, the Netherlands and Norway are seen with the fourth production aircraft for Belgium. Of these four, only the Belgian and Danish aircraft were still in service during 2001. The Dutch aircraft is now preserved: the Norwegian aircraft crashed on November 13, 1984. (Robert F Dorr collection)

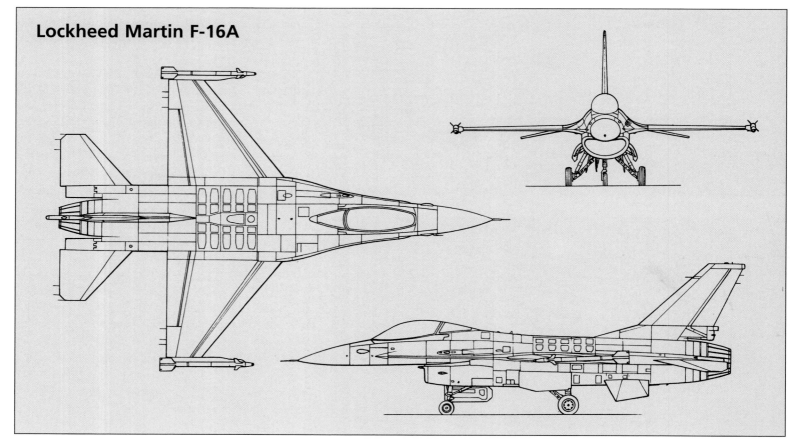

Lockheed Martin F-16A

Above: Throughout their service lives, most F-16s have received minor modifications, and other improvements. One of the most important is the Mid Life Update (MLU) programme. This photograph taken during 1990 shows the cockpit of a Danish AF F-16B several years before joining the MLU modification programme. (Ian Black)

Top right: Israel Aircraft Industries has completely refurbished the cockpit of the F-16B Avionics Capability Enhancement (ACE) demonstrator, and it now has a fully-equipped 'Glass Cockpit'. The upgrade includes three Multi-Function Displays. (KEY – Alan Warnes)

Right: Additional items gained during the conversion to MLU standard include a second Multi-Function Display on the right, together with a new wide-angle Head Up Display. (Lockheed Martin)

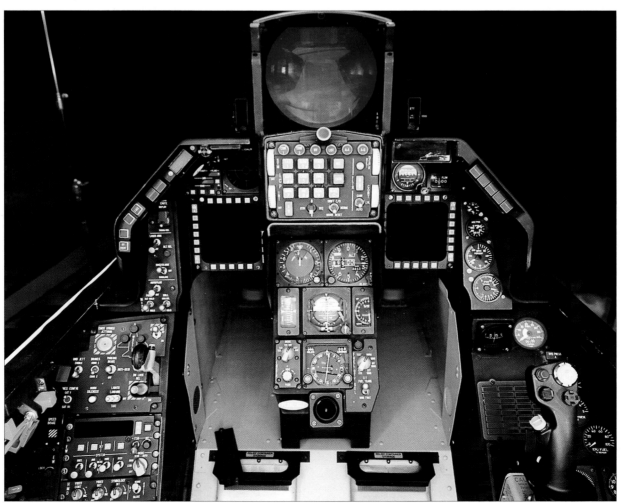

Left: An early photograph of FA-14, part of the first batch of Belgian aircraft built to Block 1 standard. This particular aircraft had a very short service life – it was lost in a mid-air collision with FA-35 over Rochefort, Belgium, on January 19, 1982. (Robert F Dorr collection)

Left: This Belgian AF F-16, FA-75, is from 23 Escadrille, part of 10 Wing based at Kleine Brogel AB. It was photographed as it performed a slow fly-by in clean configuration at the Mildenhall Air Fete in May 1990. (KEY – Duncan Cubitt)

Below left: Photographed on finals to land at RAF Waddington, Lincs, FA-102 was among the final batch of 44 aircraft for the Belgian AF and was built to Block 15 OCU standard, which introduced the ability to carry BVR missiles. (KEY – Alan Warnes)

Bottom right: Denmark purchased an initial batch of 58 F-16s. ET-205, delivered during 1980, was the second production F-16B, and was written off on December 11, 1996, while returning from a visit to RAF Marham, Norfolk. RAF air traffic control notified the crew that flames had been seen coming from the engine area on take-off. However, the crew decided to continue with the take-off run and ejected safely some 3¾ miles (5.63km) from the airfield, while flying over Narborough, Norfolk, at a height of 1,600ft (487m). The aircraft flew on for a further 8 miles (12.8km) before crashing into a sugar beet field. The student pilot had to be released from his parachute, which had become tangled in a tree. (Danish Air Force)

other front line Air Force units had rapidly begun conversion to the aircraft, allowing them to pass on their F-4Es to other active and reserve units. Egypt soon followed the Israelis, purchasing a batch of F-16s soon afterwards, initial deliveries commencing in March 1982. Following the cancellation of the low specification F-16/J-79, the door was open for more foreign countries to purchase full specification F-16As and Bs.

Initial single and two-seat versions were powered by the Pratt & Whitney F100-PW-200 afterburning turbofan. Norwegian AF aircraft were the first to be built with the tail brake parachute, a system added during upgrades by several other countries. Total Block 1 production amounted to 43 airframes, 22 of these being two-seaters.

Production then switched to the Block 5, which introduced the new grey radome. Production of this block came to 126 aircraft, of which 99 were single-seaters. Surviving Block 1 and 5 airframes were modified to Block 10 standard under a programme named 'Pacer Loft 1', which began in 1982 and ended in 1984. Block 10 production included minor systems improvements and the introduction of letters after the block number. A second Pacer Loft programme began in December 1983 and upgraded these and earlier aircraft still further.

Block 15 F-16s were the first aircraft to introduce the 'big tail', a feature which became standard on all future production aircraft. The 'big tail' has significantly more area than earlier tails, reducing the take-off rotation angle

Right: Several Belgian aircraft – including FA-81, seen here on a NATO exercise at Kecskemét, Hungary – have been modified to carry the Orpheus reconnaissance pod on the centreline pylon. (KEY – Alan Warnes)

Above: During September 2000, the Belgian AF deployed three F-16As from the 2nd Wing at Florennes to South Africa for three weeks to take part in the 80th anniversary celebrations of the South African Air Force. The three pilots also participated in the African Aerospace and Defence 2000 exhibition and airshow at Waterkloof AFB, one winning the Denel trophy for the best international solo aerobatics display. The aircrew also flew 27 sorties with the Atlas Cheetah Cs of 2 Squadron: one of these is seen leading the three F-16s over countryside near 2 Squadron's home base at Louis Trichardt. This was the first time the Belgian AF had deployed aircraft to South Africa since 1959. (BAF/Jos Keunen)

and allowing for higher angle of attack in flight. The twin blade Radar Warning Receiver (RWR) antenna under the intake was removed and placed in a new position under the radome. Some improvements were made to the radar and several changes were made to the cockpit layout, most of these resulting from a Multi Stage Improvement Programme (MSIP) introduced in 1980. MSIP Stage I improvements included various structural and wiring modifications. Most of the early survivors from the five original purchasing countries were upgraded to Block 15 standard. During the late 1980s, 241 F-16A and B Block 15s were modified for the strategic air defence role to protect North America from strategic bombers and cruise missiles, and these became known as the F-16 Air Defence Fighter (ADF). Re-equipment with these aircraft enabled the ANG to retire the McDonnell Douglas F-4C and D model Phantom IIs and the Convair F-106 Delta Darts. Modifications included upgrades to the Westinghouse AN/APG 66 radar to enable it to provide continuous wave illumination for use with AIM-7 Sparrow air-to-air missiles and to improve detection capability against small, fast-moving targets, including cruise missiles. Other improvements included the addition of a Bendix/King AN/ARC-200 HF radio – the installation of the radio antenna for this required a pair of rudder actuators to be moved down and forward, resulting in a distinctive bulge at the base of the fin. A night identification spotlight was mounted on the port side of the nose,

together with a Teledyne/E-Systems AN/APX-110 Mk XII Advanced Identification Friend or Foe (AIFF). These modifications to the rudder make the AIFF aerials the most easily-identifiable changes to this variant, with the blade antennas immediately forward of the cockpit and beneath the engine intake. Originally 270 aircraft were to be modified to ADF standard, though as the Cold War continued to thaw, only 241 aircraft were actually converted. Of these, 217 were F-16As, and the remaining 24 F-16Bs. The Oregon ANG, based at Kingsley Field, Klamath Falls, Oregon, was the first unit to receive operational ADF aircraft in March 1989, though the aircraft's service career was short due to the USAF's belief that long-range bombers and cruise missiles were no longer a threat to North America. Most of the fleet has now been retired, and only a couple of units still fly them. The aircraft retired had their ADF equipment stripped out and were flown to Davis-Monthan AFB, along with most of the surviving Block 1, 5 and 10 aircraft although, as will be described later, some of these airframes found a new lease of life elsewhere.

Mid-way through Block 15 production, the more powerful Pratt & Whitney F100-PW-220 engine was introduced, along with a new wide-angle Head-Up-Display (HUD), and this version became the Block 15 Operational Capability Upgrade (OCU). Other improvements included radar, and an avionics upgrade consisting of a combined radar-barometric altimeter, data transfer unit, increased capacity core processors and expanded software. The biggest improvements were the ability to carry AN/ALQ-119 jamming pods, and to fire next-generation Beyond Visual Range (BVR) missiles, such as the AIM-120 AMRAAM (Advanced Medium-Range Air-to-Air Missile). Newer air-to-ground weapons and a ring laser gyro Inertial Navigation System (INS) were included, along with several structural improvements. The final figure for Block 15 amounted to 983 aircraft, making this the biggest production run of all the blocks to date.

Most of the surviving Belgian, Danish, Dutch and Norwegian aircraft have been brought up to this standard, though the most ambitious upgrade for these aircraft – the F-16 Mid-Life Update (MLU) – is currently taking place. This upgrade, which initially included the USAF, brings the cockpit up to that of a current Block 50 standard aircraft, with two Honeywell liquid-crystal flat colour displays, NVG (night vision goggles) compatible lighting and wide-angle HUD, ring laser INS and navstar GPS. Also part of the package is a new modular mission computer, improved data modem, electronic warfare management system and a Hazeltine AN/APX-111 IFF, together with provision for a microwave landing system and a helmet-mounted display. All MLU aircraft now have the F100-PW-

Above: Denmark occasionally adds a splash of colour to its F-16s. E-180 is seen here at the 1999 Royal International Air Tattoo at RAF Fairford, Glos. The Danish AF was one of several countries to paint an aircraft in celebration of the 50th anniversary of NATO. (KEY – Alan Warnes)

Below: The first production F-16B ET-204 was also the first Danish aircraft to undergo the MLU conversion, and spent several years as a trials aircraft with Lockheed Martin, operating out of Edwards AFB, California, where it was photo-graphed in April 1997. It has since returned to service in Denmark. (KEY – Alan Warnes)

Above: Like most other F-16 users, Denmark often sends its F-16s to Nellis AFB, USA, to take part in Red Flag and other exercises. E-602 was photographed during one such visit in July 1993. (Ted Carlson)

220 engine fitted as standard, bringing the original four international participants' F-16s to a level similar to that of a current production F-16 Block 50/52 airframe. Several pilots have commented that this upgrade is even better than these airframes, even though they are flying a lighter, if slightly older, aircraft. Modifications also include improving the radar to AN/APG-66 (V) 2A standard, and the addition of an inlet hard-point for both these and all surviving pre-Block 15 versions, giving them the ability to carry the LANTIRN (low-altitude navigation and targeting infra-red, night) pod. F-16MLUs seem to have gained the designation F-16AM for single-seaters and F-16BM for two-seaters, and this appears to have stuck.

The final block in the F-16A and B family applies to the aircraft purchased by the Taiwanese Air Force. Originally, the Taiwanese government had been refused permission to purchase the F-16, though this changed when the People's Republic of China (PRC) began to re-equip with

Sukhoi Su-27s and became interested in purchasing Mikoyan MiG-31s to update its ageing Air Force. By the time it was given authorisation to purchase F-16s in 1992, the F-16A and B models were no longer in production. In an effort to avoid antagonising the PRC, these aircraft have been designated Block 20, despite the fact that they are actually built to late model C and D standards. They have a cockpit similar to MLU and Block 50 standards and are powered by the F100-PW-220. They are also fitted with the AN/APG-66 (V) 2 radar, and an AN/APX-111 advanced IFF as fitted to the MLU aircraft, together with AN/ALR-56M advanced radar warning receiver (ARWR) and AN/ALE-47 chaff and flare dispensers. The Taiwanese government has requested the purchase of AIM-120 AMRAAM, though this is currently being blocked by the US government.

The Jordanian, Italian, and Portuguese Air Forces have recently purchased additional airframes, mainly surplus

Right: Egypt's first batch of F-16s comprised 34 F-16As and eight F-16Bs. The second production F-16A is seen during pre-delivery manufacturer's trials at Fort Worth, following hand-over ceremonies in January 1982. First deliveries commenced in March that year. All but one of the first batch of aircraft from this order came from the Fort Worth production line, though one F-16B 81-0883, originally destined for the KLu as J-883, was diverted from the Fokker production line in Holland and became 9207. (Lockheed Martin)

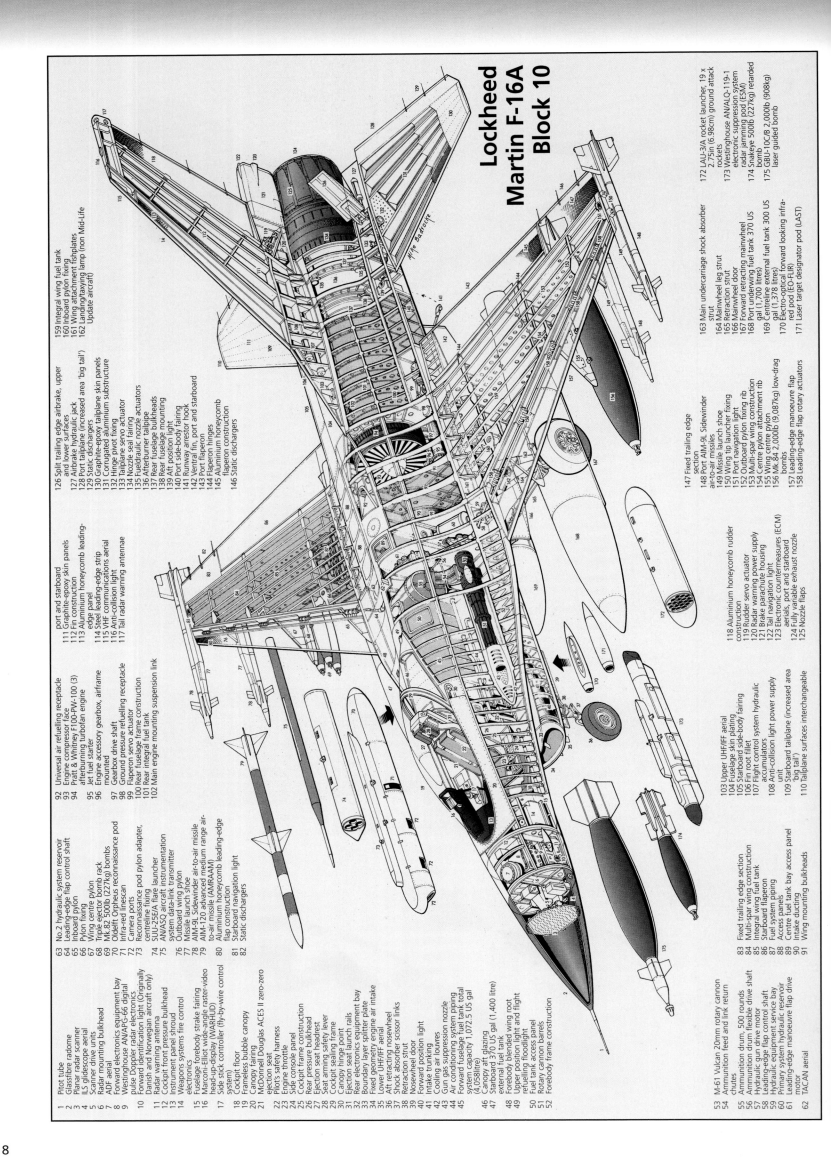

Lockheed Martin F-16A Block 10

1 Pitot tube
2 Glassfibre radome
3 Planar radar scanner
4 ILS glidescope aerial
5 Scanner drive units
6 Radar mounting bulkhead
7 ADF aerial
8 Forward electronics equipment bay
9 Westinghouse AN/APG-66 digital pulse Doppler radar electronics
10 Forward identification light (Originally Danish and Norwegian aircraft only)
11 Radar warning antenna
12 Cockpit front pressure bulkhead
13 Instrument panel shroud
14 Weapons systems fire control electronics
15 Fuselage forebody strake fairing
16 Marconi-Elliot wide-angle raster-video head-up-display (WARHUD)
17 Side stick controller (fly-by-wire control system)
18 Cockpit floor
19 Frameless bubble canopy
20 Canopy fairing
21 McDonnell Douglas ACES II zero-zero ejection seat
22 Pilot's safety harness
23 Engine throttle
24 Side console panel
25 Cockpit frame construction
26 Rear pressure bulkhead
27 Ejection seat headrest
28 Seat arming safety lever
29 Cockpit sealing frame
30 Canopy hinge point
31 Ejection seat launch rails
32 Rear electronics equipment bay
33 Boundary layer splitter plate
34 Fixed geometry engine air intake
35 Lower UHF/IFF aerial
36 Aft retracting nosewheel
37 Shock absorber scissor links
38 Retraction strut
39 Nosewheel door
40 Forward position light
41 Intake trunking
42 Cooling air louvres
43 Gun gas suppression nozzle
44 Air conditioning system piping
45 Forward fuselage fuel tank total system capacity 1,072.5 US gal (4,058litre)
46 Canopy aft glazing
47 Starboard 370 US gal (1,400 litre) external fuel tank
48 Forebody blended wing root
49 Upper position light and flight refuelling floodlight
50 Fuel tank access panel
51 Rotary cannon barrels
52 Forebody frame construction

53 M-61 Vulcan 20mm rotary cannon
54 Ammunition feed and link return chutes
55 Ammunition drum, 500 rounds
56 Ammunition drum flexible drive shaft
57 Hydraulic gun drive motor
58 Leading-edge flap drive motor
59 Hydraulic equipment service bay
60 Primary system hydraulic reservoir
61 Leading-edge manoeuvre flap drive motor
62 TACAN aerial

63 No.2 hydraulic system reservoir
64 Leading-edge flap control shaft
65 Inboard pylon
66 Pylon fixing
67 Wing centre pylon
68 Triple ejector bomb rack
69 Mk.82 500lb (227kg) bombs
70 Oldelft Orpheus reconnaissance pod
71 Infra-red linescan
72 Camera ports
73 Reconnaissance pod pylon adapter, centreline fixing
74 SUU-25E/A flare launcher
75 AN/ASQ aircraft instrumentation system data-link transmitter
76 Outboard wing pylon
77 Missile launch shoe
78 AIM-9L Sidewinder air-to-air missile
79 AIM-120 advanced medium range air-to-air missile (AMRAAM)
80 Aluminium honeycomb leading-edge flap construction
81 Starboard navigation light
82 Static dischargers

92 Universal air refuelling receptacle
93 Engine compressor face
94 Pratt & Whitney F100-PW-100 (3) afterburning turbofan engine
95 Jet fuel starter
96 Engine accessory gearbox, airframe mounted
97 Gearbox drive shaft
98 Ground pressure refuelling receptacle
99 Flaperon servo actuator
100 Rear fuselage frame construction
101 Rear integral fuel tank
102 Main engine mounting suspension link

111 port and starboard
111 Graphite-epoxy skin panels
112 Fin construction
113 Aluminium honeycomb leading-edge panel
114 Steel leading-edge strip
115 VHF communications aerial
116 Anti-collision light
117 Tail radar warning antennae

83 Fixed trailing edge section
84 Multi-spar wing construction
85 Integral wing fuel tank
86 Starboard flaperon
87 Fuel system piping
88 Access panels
89 Centre fuel tank bay access panel
90 Intake ducting
91 Wing mounting bulkheads

103 Upper UHF/IFF aerial
104 Fuselage skin plating
105 Starboard side-body fairing
106 Fin root fillet
107 Flight control system hydraulic accumulators
108 Anti-collision light power supply unit
109 Starboard tailplane (increased area 'big tail')
110 Tailplane surfaces interchangeable

126 Split trailing edge airbrake, upper and lower surfaces
127 Airbrake hydraulic jack
128 Port tailplane (increased area 'big tail')
129 Static dischargers
130 Graphite-epoxy tailplane skin panels
131 Corrugated aluminium substructure
132 Hinge pivot fixing
133 Tailplane servo actuator
134 Nozzle seal fairing
135 Fuel/hydraulic nozzle actuators
136 Afterburner tailpipe
137 Rear fuselage bulkheads
138 Rear fuselage mounting
139 Aft position light
140 Port side-body fairing
141 Runway arrestor hook
142 Ventral fin, port and starboard
143 Port flaperon
144 Flaperon hinges
145 Aluminium honeycomb flaperon construction
146 Static dischargers

159 Integral wing fuel tank
160 Inboard pylon fixing
161 Wing attachment fishplates
162 Landing/taxying lamp (non Mid-Life Update aircraft)

147 Fixed trailing edge section
148 Port AIM-9L Sidewinder air-to-air missiles
149 Missile launch shoe
150 Wing tip launcher fixing rib
151 Port navigation light
152 Outboard pylon fixing rib
153 Multi-spar wing construction
154 Centre pylon attachment rib
155 Wing centre pylon
156 Mk.84 2,000lb (9,087kg) low-drag bombs
157 Leading-edge manoeuvre flap
158 Leading-edge flap rotary actuators

118 Aluminium honeycomb rudder construction
119 Rudder servo actuator
120 Radar warning power supply
121 Brake parachute housing
122 Tail navigation light
123 Electronic countermeasures (ECM) aerials, port and starboard
124 Fully variable exhaust nozzle
125 Nozzle flaps

163 Main undercarriage shock absorber strut
164 Mainwheel leg strut
165 Retraction strut
166 Mainwheel door
167 Forward retracting mainwheel
168 Port underwing fuel tank 370 US gal (1,700 litres)
169 Centreline external fuel tank 300 US gal (1,378 litres)
170 Electro-optical forward looking infra-red pod (EO-FLIR)
171 Laser target designator pod (LAST)

172 LAU-3/A rocket launcher, 19 x 2.75in (6.98cm) ground attack rockets
173 Westinghouse AN/ALQ-119-1 electronic suppression system radar jamming pod (ESM)
174 Snakeye 500lb (227kg) retarded bomb
175 GBU-10C/8 2,000lb (908kg) laser guided bomb

Right: The first pair of Egyptian AF F-16s are seen taking on fuel from a USAF KC-135 Stratotanker on their delivery flight to Egypt in March 1982. By the end of the month, six aircraft had been delivered. Egypt has since become a regular customer for F-16s, although all subsequent orders are for the later F-16C/D model. (Lockheed Martin)

F-16 SPECIFICATIONS

Length overall:	49ft 4in (15.03m)
Wingspan:	over missile – launchers: 31ft 0in (9.45m)
Over missiles:	32ft 9¾in (10.00m)
Wing aspect ratio:	3.2
Height:	16 ft 8½in (5.09m)
Powerplant:	One Pratt & Whitney F100-PW-200
Empty weight:	18,591lb (8,433kg)
Max external load (full internal fuel):	15,930lb (7,226kg)
Maximum internal fuel:	(JP-8) 7,162lb (3,208kg)
Maximum level speed at 40,000ft (12,200m):	above M2.0
Service ceiling:	50,000ft (15,240m)
Ferry range Block 50 with 1,500 US gal (5,678 litres) external fuel:	2,276nm (4,215km)
Armament (standard air-to-air fit):	General Dynamics M61A1 20mm multi-barrel cannon in the port side wing/body fairing with 511 rounds of ammunition, 2 AIM-120 AMRAAM or AIM-9L Sidewinders, on each wingtip pylon.

ADF airframes. Italy signed an agreement with Lockheed Martin on March 15, 2001, to lease 30 Block 15 F-16ADF as part of a deal to replace former RAF Tornado F.3s on loan until the Eurofighter Typhoon enters full operational service. These Block 15 aircraft will undergo the Falcon Up upgrade. Included in the deal are four Block 10 F-16Bs, which will be upgraded to Operational Capability Upgrade status. The arrangement runs for a total of seven years as an interim replacement for the Tornados already mentioned, but the aircraft will also replace the remaining Lockheed F-104S-ASA-M Starfighters in the Italian Air Force. Air and ground crew training will take place with 162nd Fighter Squadron of the Arizona ANG at Tucson International Airport, Arizona, deliveries commencing in 2003. The contract also includes four more F-16Bs for spares use.

Right: Indonesian AF F-16s are built to Block 15 OCU standard and were delivered in this attractive three-tone blue and grey colour scheme. The first aircraft arrived in the country in December 1989, and deliveries were completed during 1990. The primary role for Indonesian F-16s is air defence armed with AIM-9P Sidewinders, though they also have a secondary air-to-ground role using AGM-65 Mavericks. (Robert F Dorr collection)

Left: As part of its 50th anniversary celebrations in 1996, the Indonesia AF formed the Elang Biru (Blue Falcons) display team. Aircrew from Skadron Udara 3 at Iswahyudi were trained by three former USAF Thunderbirds instructors, and the team performed for the first time at the Jakarta air show at Soekarno-Hatta International Airport in June 1996. The aircraft remained in this colour scheme for several years after the team was disbanded, though the Air Force has now started to repaint them in a new two-tone green and grey colour scheme. (Hendro Subroto)

Left: Since its delivery in 1980, F-16A 299 has been assigned to the Israeli AF Flight Test Centre. It was photographed at Tel Nov the day before the Independence Day airshow in May 2000. (Andy Marden)

Below: This F-16B is one of 14 of the variant transferred to the Israel AF by the USAF in 1994. With the delivery of these aircraft, the IDF/AF took the opportunity of introducing advanced training on the F-16. Students fresh from the Air Force flying school were streamed directly on to an OTU course to learn to fly them, cutting out intermediate training on a Lead-In Fighter Trainer aircraft. (Shlomo Aloni)

Above: An early four-ship formation of F-16As from 322 Squadron, which became the first operational Dutch F-16 squadron on December 31, 1979. The aircraft replaced the unit's Lockheed F-104 Starfighter. During Operation Allied Force, 322 Squadron gained the first official Netherlands Air Force kill since the Second World War. Operating out of Amendola AB in Italy, J-063 shot down a Yugoslav AF MiG-29 *Fulcrum* with an AIM-120 AMRAAM on the first night of operations. All the aircraft in this photograph have been withdrawn from active service and are currently used for ground instruction at Leeuwarden and Volkel. (Jelle Sjoerdsma collection)

Right: Another early production example, J-215, carries the badge of the Training and Conversion all-weather unit, which was initially responsible for all pilot conversion. This unit was disbanded in March 1986, the task passing to 323 Squadron until December 1989, when training was partially transferred to the 162nd Tactical Fighter Training Group (TFTG) Arizona ANG, based at Tucson International Airport, USA. A dozen KLu aircraft were flown out to the USA for this purpose, the remaining part of the training task being transferred to 316 Squadron in 1991. However, this unit only had a short existence, being disbanded on April 1, 1994. At the same time, the aircraft based in the USA returned home, and aircrew training passed to 313 Squadron at Twenthe, which still carries out the role. (KEY – Duncan Cubitt)

Apart from the F-16 MLU upgrade, two other upgrades are currently available to existing and future users of older airframes. These include the F-16 Avionics Capability Enhancement (ACE), a joint programme between Israel Aircraft Industries (IAI) and Elbit Systems which is currently undergoing testing in Israel. Also available is the Falcon One upgrade on offer from Singapore Technologies Aerospace Ltd (ST Aero), which will be developed in a joint collaboration with BAE Systems and Lockheed Martin, though at the time of writing there are currently no customers for either of these programmes.

Numerous versions of the F-16 were planned during the 1970s, and included various untried weapons fits, though most of these designs got no further than the drawing board. One version planned was a structurally-strengthened F-16A/B with a Pratt & Whitney PW1130, essentially a derivative of the existing F100 engine. Other versions proposed included one for the US Navy, which would have been designed and built by LTV Aerospace. Initially referred to as the Model 1600, this would have been a beefed-up version of the Block 10 airframe, equipped with an arrestor hook for carrier operations and a redesigned nosewheel. Several powerplants were intended for the aircraft, including the F404 (as used in the F/A-18 Hornet). The Model 1601 would have had an improved F100 engine, and the Model 1602 an F101 engine. Plans were made to arm the aircraft with AIM-7 Sparrow Air-to-Air Missiles (AAM) and to fit AIM-9 Sidewinder AAMs to launch rails on the sides of the intakes. Another design was the F-16 Swept-Forward Wing (SFW) aircraft, which was to be based on the Block 10 airframe. However, it was decided that this was too difficult to manufacture at that stage, though forward swept wing research eventually took place during the 1980s using the Grumman X-29.

Opposite page, top: No.311 Squadron is based at Volkel AB, Holland, alongside 306 and 312 Squadrons, and wears the red and white chequered fin band known as 'Brabants Bont', derived from the flag of the region. J-195 served with 311 Squadron until February 10, 1993, when it suffered technical problems returning from a mission over Germany. The pilot ejected before the aircraft crashed near a railway line north of Geffen. (Lockheed Martin)

Opposite page, centre left: Underside view of F-16A J-060 taken at the Mildenhall Air Fete. All the Dutch units take turns to perform on the airshow circuit and are known to enjoy splashing a little extra colour on their aircraft. No.315 Squadron was given the responsibility of performing during the 1990 airshow season. (KEY – Duncan Cubitt)

Opposite page, centre right: F-16B J-882 of 323 Squadron on finals to Leeuwarden in February 1998. This Squadron currently plays a Tactical Training and Evaluation Standardisation Squadron (TACTESS) role within the KLu, testing tactical aspects of new equipment. The unit became the first operational Dutch jet squadron when it converted to Gloster Meteor F.4s in 1948. (KEY – Steve Fletcher)

Opposite page, bottom: The Flight Test Centre, or Test Groep, operated from Volkel until it moved to Leeuwarden in 1999. It currently operates a modified F-16BM for test purposes, which include trials on new weapons and avionics systems. Other European operators have made use of the centre's expertise and experience.

Right: The KLu regularly uses the Canadian Forces base at Goose Bay, Labrador, for low-level flying training above the vast areas of sparsely populated land around the air base. It regularly shares ramp space with aircraft from Germany, Italy and the UK. F-16AM J-641 was photographed flying over the mountainous terrain of Greenland. (Robin Polderman)

Right: F-16A 276 performs a fast pass with afterburner at an airshow, wearing the badge of 332 Skvadron flying from Rygge AB. The Norwegian AF F-16s were the first to have the extended tail section fitted. This contains a braking parachute, essential for the short runways at some of the dispersed airfields from which the aircraft occasionally operate. (KEY – Duncan Cubitt)

Right: Norwegian F-16 squadrons have a primary role of air defence and a secondary role of anti-shipping. Norwegian aircrew wear DayGlo orange flying suits to improve visibility in the event of their having to eject over snow. Large parts of the country are very mountainous, with small valleys and fjords, as can be seen from this photo of a 334 Skvadron F-16A, based at Bodø. (Lockheed Martin)

Top: Among the participants at the 1999 Royal International Air Tattoo at RAF Fairford, Glos, was this Norwegian AF F-16B. On its arrival, it was specially painted to take part in the event's celebrations of NATO's 50th anniversary. (KEY – Alan Warnes)

Left: This 331 Skvadron F-16AM makes a sprightly departure from Ronneby, in Sweden, during Exercise Baltic Link in August 2000. The Norwegian F-16AMs operated alongside Finnish F/A-18 Hornets, and German and Polish MiG-29s, together with Swedish JA 37 Viggens and JAS 39 Gripens. (Jim Winchester)

Left: Portugal originally planned to acquire 20 F-16s from surplus USAF stocks, although it eventually opted for 20 new Block 15 OCUs to replace half its fleet of Vought A-7P Corsair IIs; the first F-16s were delivered in 1994. The first unit to receive the aircraft was Esquadra 201 and one of its F-16As is seen taxying back to its shelter at Monte Real in May 1997. Esquadra 201 operates all 20 of the first batch of F-16s, and these will eventually be joined by another squadron, yet to be named, which will operate the best of 25 ex USAF F-16 ADF airframes which arrived during 2000. All these aircraft have spent several years in desert storage at AMARC, and are currently undergoing deep maintenance with OGMA to establish the condition of the airframes. Of these 25 aircraft, only 16 F-16As and four F-16Bs will actually enter service. The five remaining F-16s will be retained for spares use. (KEY – Alan Warnes)

Right, lower right and below right: Pakistan took delivery of its first batch of F-16s in January 1983. Initially, these served with three squadrons, though one of these has since been disbanded. Plans to buy a second batch of 71 F-16s first went ahead in September 1989, though the US Congress imposed sanctions in 1990 after Pakistan refused to sign the nuclear non-proliferation treaty. A total of 28 aircraft out of the order had been completed before construction was halted, and these were flown to the Aerospace Maintenance and Regeneration Center (AMARC) at Davis-Monthan AFB, Arizona, for long-term storage, becoming the first F-16s to enter storage at the base. They have been there ever since, despite abortive attempts to sell them to countries such as the Philippines and Taiwan. A deal under which New Zealand would lease all 28 of the airframes was signed on July 28, 1999, and the process of preparing the aircraft for delivery in mid-2001 had already gone ahead when the new Labour Government in New Zealand decided to abandon the arrangement in 2000. Today the aircraft are still waiting in the desert. The latest plan would see them divided equally between the USAF (to replace older test aircraft at Edwards AFB) and the USN (for air combat training). The photographs shows four of the aircraft during a re-application of Spraylat preservative, which is applied to all aircraft entering AMARC and helps to protect them from the harsh desert climate while in storage. (KEY – Alan Warnes)

Bottom: One of the first Singaporean AF F-16Bs, seen on an early test flight from Fort Worth, devoid of its serial number. Singapore ordered four F-16As and four F-16Bs to replace the Hawker Hunter. The first aircraft, handed over on February 10, 1988, was also the 2,000th F-16 to be built, and was issued with the foreign military serial 87-0401. The Singaporean aircraft spent the first two years of their careers in full USAF colours with the 58th TFTW at Luke AFB, Arizona, until 140 Squadron was commissioned at Tengah in February 1990. The aircraft wears the old-style Singaporean Air Force insignia, which was changed from a roundel to a lion's head in the early 1990s. After the first batch of aircraft had been flown to Singapore, the Air Force decided to continue training its crews in the USA, and operated nine leased former Thunderbirds F-16As at Luke from 1993 to 1996. (Robert F Dorr collection)

left: Taiwan's F-16As and Bs were built as Block 20 models, although they are almost identical to the current Block 50 model F-16Cs and Ds. Altogether 150 aircraft have been purchased, comprising 120 F-16As and 30 F-16Bs, and these operate alongside 60 Dassault Mirage 2000-5 and 130 AIDC Ching-Kuo fighters. The Taiwanese train their F-16 aircrew at Luke AFB, Arizona, with the 21st Fighter Squadron. (KEY – Dave Allport)

Left: Thailand ordered two batches of Block 15 OCU F-16s – the first in 1987 – deliveries to 103 Squadron at Khorat commencing in 1988. The second batch was ordered in 1992, and delivered to 403 Squadron at Ta Khli in 1995 and 1996. A third squadron will form at Khorat to operate 16 ex-USAF F-16 ADFs which have been purchased and are due to arrive in 2002. Shown here is an aircraft from the first batch. (KEY – John Barker)

Below left: All four of these early production Block 5 F-16As wear the 'MC' codes of the 56th Tactical Fighter Training Wing (TFTW) based at MacDill AFB, Florida. This was the second wing to convert to the F-16, having previously flown F-4E Phantoms, and consisted of the following squadrons, three of which are represented here. At the bottom is an aircraft from the 72nd TFTS, with one from the 63rd TFTS and an example from the 61st TFTS. The final aircraft is flown by the Wing Commander: painted in the colours of all four squadrons, it wears the titles of the unit, which was re-designated as a Tactical Training Wing in 1982. The Wing later converted to F-16C and D models before being disbanded as a cost-cutting measure. The training task was consolidated with the 58th FW at Luke AFB, Arizona. (Robert F Dorr collection)

Bottom left: The third USAF Wing to convert to the F-16 was the 474th TFW, based at Nellis AFB, Nevada, another unit that fell victim to defence cutbacks at the end of the Cold War. After deactivation, the three squadrons (the 428th, 429th and 430th TFS), were reassigned to the 27th TFW at Cannon AFB, New Mexico, which operated another aircraft originating from the production line at General Dynamics, Fort Worth – the F-111 'Aardvark' long-range strike aircraft. The aircraft in this photograph, 80-0474, went on to serve with AFRes until it was retired and placed into storage at AMARC in July 1994. (Jelle Sjoerdsma collection)

Right: Another wing to convert to the F-16 after flying F-4s was the 347th TFW, based at Moody AFB, Georgia. Initially operating Block 15 F-16A/B models, it changed to the Block 40 F-16C/D LANTIRN aircraft, used by the 69th TFS during Operation Desert Storm. In 1993, two additional squadrons joined the three units seen in this photo; the 307th and 308th TFS, which moved in following the deactivation of their parent wing, the 31st TFW at Homestead AFB, Florida. (Robert F Dorr collection)

Right: The 401st TFW comprised three Tactical Fighter Squadrons based at Torrejon in Spain – the 612th 'Fighting Eagles', 613th 'Squids' and 614th 'Lucky Devils', all of which converted to Block 15 F-16s in 1983. (Robert F Dorr collection)

Right: The New Jersey Air National Guard, based at Atlantic City IAP, was the last unit to fly the Convair F-106 Delta Dart with the ANG. The unit began conversion to F-16 Block 15s in August 1988, and continued to fly them until they underwent conversion to the F-16 ADF model in 1991. (Robert F Dorr collection)

Right: The 114th Fighter Squadron has served as a training unit within the ANG for nearly 20 years, and was originally designated as a TFTS. Its main role was training aircrews for the air defence role with the ANG, initially flying F-4C Phantoms, though it exchanged these in 1988 for the F-16 Block 15. It received the first F-16ADF in 1989. (Robert F Dorr collection)

Above: In 1990, this Block 15 F-16B became the first aircraft to fly from Fort Worth with the improved Pratt & Whitney F100-PW-229 engine. (Robert F Dorr collection)

Left: A small number of the F-16 ADF variants were still in service with three ANG units in 2001. This aircraft is from the 184th FS Arkansas ANG, based at Fort Smith Military Airport (MAP). The 184th FS converted to the F-16C/D in 2001. (KEY – Alan Warnes)

Left: F-16As from three Florida-based units. The lead aircraft is from the 159th FS Florida ANG, based at Jacksonville IAP: the other two were based at Homestead AFB, Florida. The aircraft nearest the camera is from the 93rd FS/482nd TFW AFRes, and the other from the 31st TFW. (Robert F Dorr collection)

Left: The Venezuelan AF was the first South American air force to operate the F-16. It ordered them in 1982, and deliveries of the first six began in November 1983. The Venezuelan AF also had the distinction of becoming the first Latin American country to participate in Red Flag exercises at Nellis AFB. Plans to upgrade the fleet to MLU standard have not yet come to fruition, and nor have attempts to purchase a pair of F-16Bs to replace two lost in accidents. Both schemes are still awaiting funding. (Robert F Dorr collection)

In 1980, the USAF implemented the Multi-national Staged Improvement Programme (MSIP), which enabled any future systems under development or in the planning stage to be easily integrated into the airframe at a later date. The first MSIP aircraft made its first flight on December 14, 1982, and the production aircraft were given the designation F-16C and F-16D. Block designation for the new models started at 25.

External differences included a larger fin root to accommodate the ITT/Westinghouse ALQ-165 Airborne Self-Protection Jammer (ASPJ) originally planned for all USAF F-16Cs. However, the USAF withdrew from this programme during 1990, due to delays and budget overruns. All F-16C/D models have a UHF radio blade antennae at the forward base of the vertical fin, together with internal changes which included an APG-68 radar offering improved resolution and greater range, plus more expanded modes of operation compared to the earlier APG-66. An updated and more advanced cockpit featured multi-function displays, and a GEC Avionics wide-angle Head-Up Display (HUD).

This was the first time these had been used on F-16s, as apart from upgrades, the A and B models had never had them fitted. Also included were increased capacity electrical and air conditioning systems, improved computer processors, and structural improvements to enable the aircraft to operate at higher take-off weights and manoeuvring limits. Provision was made to carry AGM-65D Maverick and AIM-120 AMRAAM, and this Block also carries two ALE-40 chaff and flare dispensers.

The first production F-16C (83-1118) flew on June 15, 1984; followed on September 14 by the first F-16D. Block 25 F-16s were delivered with the F100-PW-200 engine, which experienced some initial teething troubles as the engines lacked a digital electronic engine control (DEEC). Remedial action was taken by fitting the new build F100-

Below: The Bahrain Amiri Air Force received its first batch of F-16s in March 1990. Twelve aircraft were purchased for use alongside Northrop F-5 Tiger IIs: the order was for eight F-16Cs with the rest built as F-16Ds. This aircraft is the first production F-16D. (Lockheed Martin)

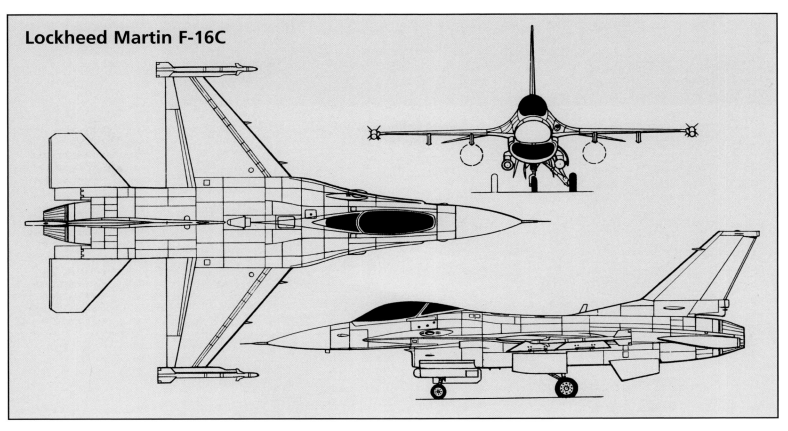

Lockheed Martin F-16C

Left: Egypt operates the fourth largest fleet of F-16s. Apart from an earlier purchase of 42 F-16A/Bs; all its subsequent orders have been for the F-16C/D model. Pictured here is the second production F-16C, from the first batch of F-16C and Ds built to Block 32 standard. All the remaining aircraft purchased by Egypt have been built as Block 40. The Block 32 airframes have since been upgraded to full Block 40 standard in a programme begun in the 1990s. Of the five batches purchased, all but one was built at Fort Worth – this was manufactured by TUSAS in Turkey. (Lockheed Martin)

Left: Greece placed its first order for 42 F-16s in November 1984, though the contract was not signed until early 1987. Deliveries of the first production aircraft to the squadrons at Nea Ankhiolos commenced in January 1989. This pair of aircraft is seen taxying out at Nea Ankhiolos for a practice bombing mission in July 1995. (KEY – Alan Warnes)

Left: F-16s in Israeli Air Force service are known by Hebrew names: F-16Cs are called *Barak* (Lightning) and F-16Ds are *Brakeet* (Thunderbolt). Israel was the first country to use its F-16Ds as a dedicated strike aircraft rather than simply as a two-seat combat conversion trainer. This F-16C sits under a shelter awaiting its next mission. (KEY – Alan Warnes)

Left: South Korea became the first export customer for the F-16C/D model, initially purchasing a batch of 36 aircraft. Deliveries of 30 F-16Cs and six F-16Ds began in 1986, and were followed in 1988 by a small top-up order for four F-16Ds. Four early production aircraft are seen flying over the Olympic stadium and village in Seoul during the 1988 Olympic Games in South Korea. (Lockheed Martin)

Top: Turkey operates a large fleet of F-16s, all built under licence by Turkish Aerospace Industries (TAI) in Ankara. This, the first production airframe, initially served with 141 Filo (Squadron) at Murted AB, since renamed Akinci. (KEY – Archive)

Above: The 527th Aggressor Squadron flew the F-16 for only a short time, converting to Block 30s in early 1989. The unit had previously flown the Northrop F-5E Tiger II as the 527th Tactical Fighter and Training Aggressor Squadron from RAF Alconbury, Cambridge-shire. However, prior to its conversion to F-16s, the unit moved to RAF Bentwaters, Suffolk, join-ing the based 81st TFW in the process. The Squadron Commander's aircraft is pictured here outside one of the Hardened Aircraft Shelters (HAS). The squadron was disbanded in 1990 when the USAF decided to disestablish all of its aggressor squadrons as a result of major post-Cold War cutbacks. (USAF)

PW-220, or the 220E, which had been converted from an existing F100-PW-200 engine. These were the last mod-els built for which Pratt & Whitney still had the monopoly of producing F-16 engines.

One F-16D Block 25, 84-1330, was used for a number of reconnaissance trials at Edwards during the 1980s, and although this was never actually given the designation RF-16D, it carried a large pod on the centreline containing various systems, making its last flight with this on August 19, 1986. Lack of interest was the main reason the pro-gramme was discontinued, although during the late 1990s, interest revived.

Another early model F-16 Block 25 which has spent most of its life being used in various trials is F-16C 83-1120, which initially served as the trials airframe for the Alternative Engine Programme. As such it was used to test the General Electric F110 engine, together with the modular common inlet duct. This aircraft also served as the trials test-bed for the F-16 Extended Strategic (ES), development of which began during 1994 as a proposal for Israel and included the addition of two blended Conformal Fuel Tanks (CFT) attached to the upper sides of the fuselage. Later in the testing phase, a nose-mounted FLIR was installed in the aircraft, one above the nose, and the other beneath the nose in front of the intake. The air-craft first flew in this configuration on November 3, 1994, and trials were completed in January 1995, when it was de-modified and returned to test duties at Edwards.

In 1984, the USAF had decided on the Alternative Engine Programme, which gave it the choice of two pow-

erplants for all future F-16s. The two engines were the General Electric F110-GE-100 series for Blocks 30/40/50, and the Pratt & Whitney F100-PW-220 series for Blocks 32/42/52. The most significant change to the Block 30 family was the introduction of the configured or common engine bay, which had the capacity to accommodate both Pratt & Whitney and General Electric engines. In reality, this was not as simple as it sounds, due to the need for a modification kit, which was only available at depot level. The engine bays have appropriate mountings, though they lack the actuator rods and cables to make inter-changing engines practical. As a result, the USAF does not swap engines, but splits different powered aircraft into squadrons or wings. It also keeps GE-powered air-craft overseas and PW-engined aircraft based at home.

Block 30s were the first production aircraft to be pow-ered by the General Electric F110-GE-100 engines, which means that they are fitted with the larger air intake. Block 30s also have additional weapons capabilities, including the ability to fire the AIM-120 AMRAAM and the AGM-45 Shrike anti radiation missile. Some avionics changes were added, including a crashworthy flight-data recorder and a voice message unit: seal-bonded centre and aft fuselage fuel tanks were also installed. The aircraft carry two ALE-47 chaff/flare dispensers, although for those starting in fiscal year 1987, this number has been dou-bled. F-16 Block 30s for Greece and Turkey were built with the extended fairing at the base of the tail for the braking parachute. Greek aircraft also have the identifica-tion light in the nose.

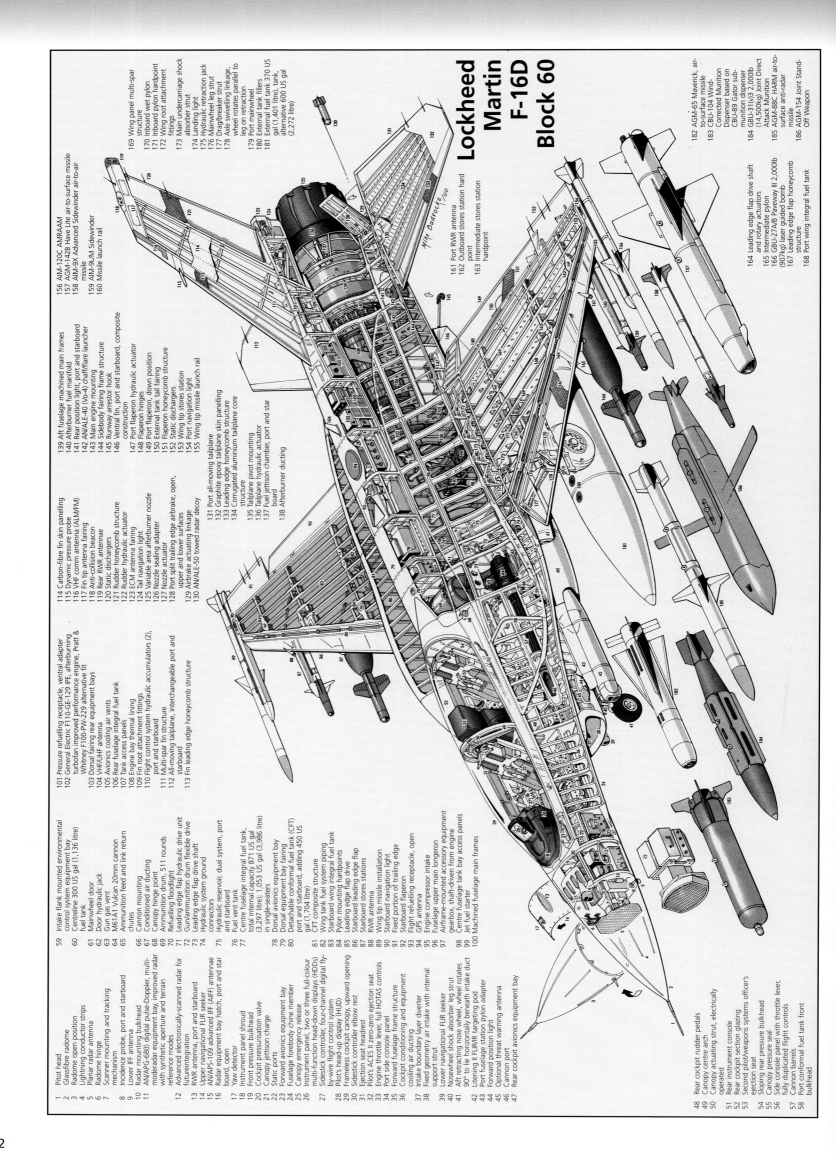

Lockheed Martin F-16D Block 60

1 Pitot head
2 Glassfibre radome
3 Radome open position
4 Lightning conductor strips
5 Planar radar antenna
6 Radome hinge
7 Scanner mounting and tracking mechanism
8 Incidence probe, port and starboard
9 Lower IFF antenna
10 Radar mounting bulkhead
11 AN/APG-68(l) digital pulse-Doppler, multi-moderadar equipment bay, improved radar with synthetic aperture and terrain reference modes
12 Advanced electronically-scanned radar for futureintegration
13 Upper navigational FLIR seeker
14 RWR antenna, port and starboard
15 AN/APS-109 advanced IFF (AIFF) antennae
16 Radar equipment bay hatch, port and starboard, open
17 Yaw detector
18 Instrument panel shroud
19 Front pressure bulkhead
20 Cockpit pressurisation valve
21 Canopy jettison charge
22 Static ports
23 Forward avionics equipment bay
24 Fuselage forebody chine member
25 Canopy emergency release
26 Instrument panel, two or three full-colour multi-function head-down displays (HDDs)
27 Sidestick controller, four-channel digital fly-by-wire flight control system
28 Pilot's head-up display (HUD)
29 Frameless cockpit canopy, upward opening
30 Sidestick controller elbow rest
31 Ejection seat headrest
32 Pilot's ACES II zero-zero ejection seat
33 Engine throttle lever, full HOTAS controls
34 Port side console panel
35 Forward fuselage frame structure
36 Cockpit conditioning and equipment cooling air ducting
37 Intake boundary layer diverter
38 Fixed geometry air intake with internal support strut
39 Lower navigational FLIR seeker
40 Nosewheel shock absorber leg strut
41 Aft retracting nose wheel, wheel rotates 90° to lie horizontally beneath intake duct
42 Litening II FLIR/IR targeting pod
43 Port fuselage station pylon adapter
44 Forward position light
45 Optional threat warning antenna
46 Cannon port
47 Rear cockpit avionics equipment bay
48 Rear cockpit rudder pedals
49 Canopy centre arch
50 Canopy actuating strut, electrically operated
51 Rear instrument console
52 Rear cockpit section glazing
53 Second pilot/weapons systems officer's ejection seat
54 Sloping rear pressure bulkhead
55 Canopy pressure seal
56 Side console panel with throttle lever, fully duplicated flight controls
57 Cannon barrels
58 Port conformal fuel tank front bulkhead

59 Intake flank mounted environmental control system equipment bay
60 Centreline 300 US gal (1,136 litre) fuel tank
61 Mainwheel door
62 Door hydraulic jack
63 Gun gas vent
64 M61A1 Vulcan 20mm cannon
65 Ammunition feed and link return chutes
66 Cannon mounting
67 Conditioned air ducting
68 Canopy hinge point
69 Ammunition drum, 511 rounds
70 Refuelling floodlight
71 Leading edge flap hydraulic drive unit
72 Gun/ammunition drum flexible drive
73 Leading edge flap drive shaft
74 Hydraulic system ground connectors
75 Hydraulic reservoir, dual system, port and starboard
76 Fuel vent tank
77 Centre fuselage integral fuel tank, total internal capacity 871 US gal (3,297 litre); 1,053 US gal (3,986 litre) in single-seaters
78 Dorsal avionics equipment bay
79 Dorsal equipment bay fairing
80 Detachable conformal fuel tank (CFT) port and starboard, adding 450 US gal (1,704 litre)
81 CFT composite structure
82 Wing tank fuel system piping
83 Starboard wing integral fuel tank
84 Pylon mounting hardpoints
85 Leading edge flap drive
86 Starboard leading edge flap
87 Starboard stores stations
88 RWR antenna
89 Wing tip missile installation
90 Starboard navigation light
91 Fixed portion of trailing edge
92 Starboard flaperon
93 Flight refuelling receptacle, open
94 GPS antenna
95 Engine compressor intake
96 Fuselage upper main longeron
97 Airframe-mounted accessory equipment gearbox, shaft-driven from engine
98 Centre fuselage tank bay access panels
99 Jet fuel starter
100 Machined fuselage main frames

101 Pressure refuelling receptacle, ventral adapter
102 General Electric F110-GE-129 IPE, afterburning turbofan improved performance engine; Pratt & Whitney F100-PW-229 alternative fit
103 Dorsal fairing rear equipment bays
104 VHF/UHF antenna
105 Avionics cooling air vents
106 Rear fuselage integral fuel tank
107 Tank access panels
108 Engine bay thermal lining
109 Fin root attachment fittings
110 Flight control system hydraulic accumulators (2), port and starboard
111 Multi-spar fin structure
112 All-moving tailplane, interchangeable port and starboard
113 Fin leading edge honeycomb structure
114 Carbon-fibre fin skin panelling
115 Dynamic pressure probe
116 VHF comm antenna (ALMFM)
117 Fin tip antenna fairing
118 Anti-collision beacon
119 Rear RWR antennae
120 Static dischargers
121 Rear fuselage honeycomb structure
122 Rudder hydraulic actuator
123 ECM antenna fairing
124 Tail navigation light
125 Variable area afterburner nozzle
126 Nozzle sealing adapter
127 Nozzle actuator
128 Port split trailing edge airbrake, open, upper and lower surfaces
129 Airbrake actuating linkage
130 AN/ALE-50 towed radar decoy
131 Port all-moving tailplane
132 Graphite epoxy tailplane skin panelling
133 Leading edge honeycomb structure
134 Corrugated aluminium tailplane core structure
135 Tailplane pivot mounting
136 Tailplane hydraulic actuator
137 Fuel jettison chamber, port and star board
138 Afterburner ducting
139 Aft fuselage machined main frames
140 Afterburner fuel manifold
141 Rear position light, port and starboard
142 AN/ALE-40 (Vo-4) chaff/flare launcher
143 Main engine mounting
144 Sidebody fairing frame structure
145 Runway arrestor hook
146 Ventral fin, port and starboard, composite construction
147 Port flaperon hydraulic actuator
148 Flaperon hinges
149 Port flaperon, down position
150 External tank tail fairing
151 Flaperon honeycomb structure
152 Static dischargers
153 Wing tip stores station
154 Port navigation light
155 Wing tip missile launch rail
156 AIM-120C AMRAAM
157 AGM-142B Have Lite air-to-surface missile
158 AIM-9X Advanced Sidewinder air-to-air missile
159 AIM-9L/M Sidewinder
160 Missile launch rail
161 Port RWR antenna
162 Outboard stores station hard point
163 Intermediate stores station hardpoint
164 Leading edge flap drive shaft and rotary actuators
165 Intermediate pylon
166 GBU-27A/B Paveway III 2,000lb (907kg) laser guided bomb
167 Leading edge flap honeycomb structure
168 Port wing integral fuel tank
169 Wing panel multi-spar structure
170 Inboard wet pylon
171 Inboard pylon hardpoint
172 Wing root attachment fittings
173 Main undercarriage shock absorber strut
174 Landing light
175 Hydraulic retraction jack
176 Mainwheel leg strut
177 Dragbreaker strut
178 Axle swivelling linkage, wheel rotates parallel to leg on retraction
179 Port mainwheel
180 External tank fillers
181 External fuel tank 370 US gal (1,401 litre), tank, alternative 600 US gal (2,272 litre)
182 AGM-65 Maverick, air-to-surface missile
183 CBU-104 Wind-Corrected Munition Dispenser based on CBU-89 Gator sub-munition dispenser
184 GBU-31(v)3 2,000lb (14,500kg) Joint Direct Attack Munition
185 AGM-88C HARM air-to-surface anti-radar missile
186 AGM-154 Joint Stand-Off Weapon

F-16C BLOCK 50 DATA	
Length overall:	49ft 4in (15.03m)
Wingspan:	over missile launchers: 31ft 0in (9.45m)
Over missiles:	32ft 9¾in (10.00m)
Wing aspect ratio:	3.2
Height::	16ft 8½in (5.09m)
Powerplant::	One General Electric F110-GE-129 or Pratt & Whitney F100-PW-129 Increased performance engine (IPE)
Empty weight:	F100-PW-119: 18,591lb (8,433kg)
Empty weight:	F110-GE-129: 18,917lb (8,581kg)
Max external load: (full internal fuel)	F100-PW-119: 15,930lb (7,226kg)
Max external load: (full internal fuel)	F110-GE-129: 15,591lb (7,072kg)
Maximum internal fuel:	(JP-8) 7,162lb (3,208kg)
Maximum level speed :	above M2.0 at 40,000ft (12,200m)
Service ceiling:	50,000ft (15,240m) at 40,000ft (12,200m)
Radius of action (combat air patrol mission):	ferry range Block 50 with 1,500 US gals (5,678 litres) external fuel 2,276nm (4,215km)
Armament (a-a):	General Dynamics M61A1 20mm multi-barrel cannon in the port side wing/body fairing with 511 rounds of ammunition, two AIM-120 AMRAAMs or AIM-9L Sidewinders, on each wingtip pylon.

Above: The 138th FS, New York ANG, currently operates F-16 Block 25s from Hancock Field, Syracuse. Both the aircraft illustrated here are carrying AN/ALQ-184 ECM pods and AIM-9 Sidewinders during a Red Flag training mission over the Nevada desert. (Rick Llinares)

Right: Most of the earlier Block 25 and Block 30 airframes still in service with the USAF have been transferred to the Air National Guard (ANG), while others have been assigned to various training units. The Arizona ANG is responsible for training aircrews for both the ANG and AFRC, and as such reports to Air Education and Training Command (AETC). The three squadrons assigned to the wing operate all four versions of F-16s, while the separate unit – the ANG and AFRC Test Center – also carries out trials work. (KEY Archive)

The first Block 30 F-16C (85-1398) flew on June 12, 1986, followed by F-16D (85-1509) on July 30. Turkish F-16C Block 30 have been fitted with Loral AN/ALQ-178 ECM (earlier production aircraft have since had this added). Greek aircraft have also been equipped with the Advanced Self Protection Integrated Suite (ASPIS), which adds new radar warning receivers, and an internal AN/ALQ-187 jammer, linked to the countermeasures.

The US Navy also purchased a batch of Block 30 aircraft for aggressor training, although these only carried the original APG-66 radar instead of the APG-68. Numerous modifications for this role included a strengthened airframe and titanium lower wing fittings, together with radar reflectors fitted to the intake sides, enhancing the aircraft's cross-section. The M61A1 cannon was deleted to save weight and the aircraft had no ability to carry weapons, other than acquisition rounds for the AIM-9 and the AIS instrumentation pod for air combat. The US Navy gave the aircraft the following designations – F-16N for the single-seat and TF-16N for the two-seat. The first F-16N (85-1369/USN Bureau No.163268) flew on March 24, 1987. F-16Ns had a very brief service career – they were retired in 1994 and had been completely removed from service by 1995 for financial reasons, which included cutbacks in aggressor training. This was a great shame as they were the most manoeuvrable variants in the whole F-16 family, their reduced weight making them excellent dogfighters.

Israel had already purchased earlier models of the F-16A and B, and soon selected the Block 30 to replace IAI Kfirs and McDonnell Douglas A-4 Skyhawks, together with some F-4 Phantoms. Included in these orders were a high proportion of F-16Ds, which were built with large humps on the spine: these are filled with extra avionics for operational missions. Block 32 F-16s are essentially similar to the Block 30 airframes, except that this Block saw the introduction of the wing-mounted radar warning receiver (RWR) which replaced two blade aerials on the nose of earlier aircraft. Relocating these gives the front of the aircraft better coverage, and this system has since been refitted to all other USAF F-16C and Ds. The first flights of both a single and twin-seat Block 32 took place on the same day – June 12, 1986, when F-16C (86-0210)

Left: Torrejon's 401st TFW converted to Block 30 F-16s in 1989 and the three Squadrons within the Wing frequently deployed to other airfields for training. One of these was Incirlik, in Turkey, where the Wing Commander's aircraft was photographed. In 1991, the 614th TFS moved to Doha AB in Qatar to take part in Operation Desert Storm, afterwards returning to Torrejon. This was only for a short period, however, as the Spanish government had voted to remove all US combat units from its soil. Plans were made to relocate the unit to a brand new air base at Crotone in Italy, though by the end of 1991 these had been abandoned and the wing de-activated. (KEY – Duncan Cubitt)

Left: During 1987, the 52nd TFW at Spangdahlem, Germany, commenced conversion to the Block 30 model, replacing its McDonnell Douglas F-4E Phantoms. One of the three original squadrons within the Wing was the 81st TFS and one of the unit's aircraft is seen here on finals to land at RAF Mildenhall, Suffolk. Each of the units operated a mix of F-4Gs and F-16s in the SEAD role, initially carrying the AGM-45 Shrike Anti-Radiation Missile. (KEY-Duncan Cubitt)

Left: The 86th Tactical Fighter Wing at Ramstein was another USAFE Wing which converted from the Phantom, though unlike most other units in Germany, the 86th TFW had only two squadrons attached to it – the 512th TFS 'Dragons' and the 526th TFS 'Black Knights'. The latter began conversion to F-16s during 1985, flying Block 30s until 1993 when it converted to Block 40 airframes. Both units moved to Aviano, Italy, to form the 31st FW in autumn 1993, leaving the renamed 86th Airlift Wing (AW) to operate a mix of transport types. (Mike Rondot collection)

Below: The VISTA F-16D is a highly-modified aircraft which has taken part in a number of research programmes, including the Multi Axis Thrust Vectoring (MATV) trials, during which it was refitted with an anti-spin recovery parachute. After completing the thrust vectoring experiments, it went on to serve as a trials aircraft for new combat aircraft, including the Lockheed Martin F-35 Joint Strike Fighter (JSF). (Lockheed Martin)

Bottom: Almost all the F-16s built have emerged from the Lockheed Martin production line at Fort Worth, Texas. Located across the other side of the runway is Fort Worth Joint Reserve Base (JRB), once formerly known as Carswell AFB, which is home to a number of units, including the 457th FS (AFRC), which now flies F-16 Block 30s. One of its Block 25 F-16Cs is pictured returning from a mission in October 1995. (KEY – Alan Warnes)

flew first, followed by F-16D (86-0039). Some of these aircraft were delivered to the 302nd FS (AFRes) based at Luke AFB Arizona, and these became the first models of the newer F-16s to be issued to the reserve forces.

The USAF, US Navy and NASA funded a single Block 30 F-16D 86-0048 for research into new and modified aircraft designs. This aircraft gained the designation NF-16D, denoting that it is modified to a certain configuration for test purposes only. It first flew as the Variable-Stability In-Flight Simulator Test Aircraft (VISTA) on April 9, 1992. The VISTA is modified to act as an airborne simulator, and with the aid of flying control computers it can simulate the flight characteristics of other high performance aircraft and airliners by means of a centre control stick in addition to the normal sidestick found on all other F-16s. It has also been fitted out to enable the aircraft commander to sit in the rear cockpit. VISTA served in this role throughout 1992 and early 1993 before it was modified to serve as the Multi Axis Thrust Vectoring (MATV) trials aircraft. These trials required the F110 engine to be fitted with a new exhaust nozzle designated the Axisymmetric Vectoring Exhaust Nozzle (AVEN): the aircraft made its first flight in this form on July 2, 1993. Fitted out in this configuration, it undertook high angle of attack, and pitch and yaw thrust vectoring.

Israel originally supported the concept, intending to fit the AVEN nozzle in all its F-16s. The Israeli AF had planned to supply an aircraft to undertake the testing phase for this, though later Israel withdrew from the proj-

ect on cost grounds. This left just the USAF and Lockheed, to enable the programme to go ahead, some of the variable stability computers installed while the aircraft served as VISTA were removed, restoring the airframe to almost the weight of a normal F-16. After these trials were completed, the aircraft undertook more experimental technology work in the form of Advanced Control Technology for Integrated Vehicles (ACTIVE) for both NASA and the USAF at Edwards AFB, between October and November 1994. Following completion of these tests, it was transferred to the Calspan Corporation at Wright Patterson AFB, Ohio, where it replaced a long-serving NT-33A Shooting Star as a variable stability flight demonstrator. There a Pratt & Whitney engine was installed, and it was converted back to the VISTA configuration in January 1995. It has since been used by the Air Force Flight Test Center and Lockheed Martin for various trials replicating the flight characteristics of advanced aircraft such as the Lockheed Martin F-22 and both the Joint Strike Fighter prototypes. VISTA has also performed trials for NASA's X-38 space shuttle and international space station crew return vehicle. In October 2000, the airframe was finally transferred to the USAF Test Pilots School (TPS) to enable students to simulate flight in a broad range of other aircraft.

With the retirement of the McDonnell Douglas RF-4C Phantom II in October 1995, the ANG found itself without a manned tactical reconnaissance asset. In March 1995, the USAF Chief of Staff had requested that the

Left: New Mexico's ANG unit is the 188th FS, assigned to the 150th FW based at Kirtland AFB, near Albuquerque, New Mexico. The unit is tasked with two missions, one the Fast FAC (Forward Air Controller) mission. The other half of the squadron's role is designated as a Defence Systems Evaluation (DSE) detachment which supports the US Army weapons range at White Sands, also in New Mexico. The aircraft act as simulated targets for Surface-to-Air Missiles (SAM) and perform other missions as part of ongoing Army Research and Development (R&D). Aircraft assigned to this role have a black fin tip like this Block 30 F-16D, photographed on the flightline at Kirtland in 1995. (KEY – Alan Warnes)

Left: All the remaining New Mexico ANG aircraft wear yellow fin tips, as seen on this pair of Block 40 F-16Cs, flying through Monument Valley in Arizona. Both aircraft are specially painted, with the Squadron's titles on the nearest aircraft and the Group or Wing title on the other. (Lockheed Martin)

ANG be able to field an initial reconnaissance capability by the time the RF-4s were retired. Trials of a development pod had taken place at Edwards AFB in 1986, using an F-16D, although interest in this system was subsequently shelved. By 1995, however, the Danish company Per Udsen was developing a new pod known as the Modular Reconnaissance Pod (MRP) for the Danish Air Force, which would enable the Danes to replace the Red Baron system taken from Saab J 35 Drakens retired during 1993.

The MRP pod was evaluated for possible use by the Arizona ANG, and further trials took place with the 192nd FG/Virginia ANG, based at Richmond International Airport. Systems evaluated included Lockheed's own one-off EO-1 pod, which underwent trials between April and June 1995. The next system to undergo trials was named simply 'the Richmond recce pod'. Though similar to the EO-1, it used digital technology instead of traditional 'wet' film. The third and final pod to be evaluated is now known as the AN/ASD-11 Theater Airborne Reconnaissance System (TARS), built by Lockheed Martin Fairchild Systems. Various sensors were mounted in a pod on the aircraft's centreline stores station, the pod being produced with co-operation from Terma Electronika AS of Denmark. A total of five ANG wings flying Block 30 airframes will gain a secondary reconnaissance mission, while still retaining their air-to-ground capability. To fur-

ther enhance this role, ANG and Air Force Reserve Command (AFRC) aircraft are being modified to carry the Rafael Litening II pod, which is being licence-built in the USA by Northrop Grumman.

With the introduction into service of the Block 40/42, the F-16 gained a true night-adverse weather capability via Lockheed Martin's LANTIRN twin-podded system. The two pods include the AN/AAQ-13 navigation pod, located on the port chin, and an AN/AAQ-14 targeting pod carried on the starboard chin station. Other improvements included a stronger landing gear to cope with increased air-to-ground loads. Larger wheels, tyres and brakes were introduced from these blocks onwards, together with undercarriage doors with slightly more prominent bulges. An important change to these aircraft concerned the landing lights, which had previously been located on the main undercarriage legs. The aircraft's capability to carry chin-mounted sensor pods interfered with these lights, and so the landing lights were relocated onto the nosewheel door. Other additions included the improved AN/APG-68V radar and a different HUD, a digital flight control system, automatic terrain-following capability and provisions for Global Positioning Systems (GPS). Another feature introduced to the Block 40/42 was the Combat Edge pressure-breathing system for increased pilot g tolerance. The aircraft can also receive digitally transferred targeting data from Forward Air Controllers

Right: A pair of 184th FW Kansas ANG F-16 Block 25s from McConnell AFB, Kansas, are seen escorting a Rockwell B-1B Lancer from the 28th BS, 384th BW, also from McConnell. The Kansas ANG became the second ANG unit responsible for aircrew training, following the Arizona ANG. Three squadrons were assigned to the Wing, the 127th, 161st and the 177th FS, which initially used F-16 Block 10 airframes. However, the 127th FS converted to Block 25 F-16s in 1990/91 and continued to operate F-16s until some B-1s were passed on to the ANG. When the 384th BW de-activated on July 1, 1994, the B-1s moved down the airfield and the 127th FS became the 127th BS, 184th BW. (Rockwell)

Above: Colorado ANG F-16s carry the legend 'Mile High Militia' honouring the 'Minutemen', the militia who promised to be ready to fight in the American War of Independence 'at a moment's notice'. The aircraft was photographed during Airshow Down Under at Avalon, New South Wales, during March 1995. The Australians have also 'zapped' this Block 30 aircraft with a small DayGlo kangaroo sticker just visible on the intake. (Richard Siudak)

(FAC). Information can be received from other aircraft, such as the Boeing E-8C JSTARS (Joint Surveillance & Target Attack Radar Systems) or the Boeing RC-135 Rivet Joint reconnaissance aircraft, while operating over the battlefield. The first Block 40 F-16C 87-0350 flew on December 23, 1988, with the first F-16D, 87-0391, following on February 8, 1989. Meanwhile, the first production Block 42 F-16C 87-0356 flew on April 25, 1989, and F-16D 87-0394 made its first flight a month later, on May 26.

The two current versions available from the Fort Worth production line are the Block 50 and 52, both of which have the latest uprated engines. Block 50s are powered by the General Electric F110-GE-129, while the Block 52 uses the Pratt & Whitney F100-PW-229 version: both engines are referred to as Increased Performance Engines (IPE). Other upgrades include the AN/APG-68V5 radar featuring advanced signal processing capabilities, and the

AN/ALR-56M advanced RWR system which works together with the improved AN/ALE-47 Group A chaff flare/dispenser system. The USAF aircraft have the provision for LANTIRN, though at present they do not have the necessary software as they are used in the Suppression of Enemy Air Defences (SEAD) role. For this, they are fitted with the AN/ASQ-213 HARM Targeting System (HTS) pod (attached to the right sensor station on the intake), which provides range and direction information to guide AGM-88 anti radiation missiles to the relevant target.

Most international Block 50/52 users have the LANTIRN capability for their F-16s. They do not have the HARM Targeting System, though they retain the ability to carry and fire the HARM. Korean aircraft are being fitted with the internal AN/ALQ-165 Airborne Self-Protection Jammer System (ASPJ) and have been cleared to operate with the AGM-84 Harpoon anti-ship missile capability. Since July 2000, Block 50 aircraft have been delivered

Above: F-16s from all three squadrons assigned to the 388th FW can be seen in this photo. The nearest aircraft carries the colours of all three units on the tail fin flash: behind it are two aircraft from the 421st FS, followed by two 34th FS and finally a single 4th FS aircraft, with the Uinta Mountains, Utah, as a backdrop. (KEY – Alan Warnes)

Above: Luke AFB, Arizona, houses eight squadrons: two units are dedicated to training Singaporean and Taiwanese AF students. Three of the USAF squadrons currently use F-16 Block 25s, the remaining three flying Block 42s. In place of a previous loan agreement which utilised USAF aircraft, the Taiwanese keep some 20 of their own Block 20 airframes at Luke, while the Singaporeans now operate 16 of their Block 52s. (KEY – Alan Warnes)

Left: By late 2001, the 27th Fighter Wing at Cannon AFB, near Clovis, New Mexico, had been flying General Dynamics' products for 32 years. It converted to the F-111 in 1969 and flew all the versions operated by the USAF, though it only flew the FB-111A in a modified F-111G form. The wing finally began conversion to the F-16 Block 30 in 1995, and three squadrons now fly a mix of Block 30 and 40 airframes. A fourth unit trains Singaporean AF crews, fresh from conversion training at Luke, in advanced flying and weapons techniques. (KEY – Alan Warnes)

Bottom: F-16Ns had a short career with the US Navy, serving with only four units. Two of these were with the US Atlantic fleet: VF-43, 'The Challengers' at Naval Air Station (NAS) Oceana, Virginia, and VF-45 'Blackbirds' at NAS Key West, Florida. The two Pacific fleet units, VF-126 'Bandits', and the Naval Fighter Weapons School (NFWS), popularly known as Top Gun, were based at NAS Miramar, California. All four squadrons were deactivated when the aircraft were retired, though the NFWS still survives as part of the Naval Strike and Air Warfare Center (NSAWC) at NAS Fallon, Nevada. (Robert F Dorr collection)

with an On-Board Oxygen Generating System (OBOGS), a modular mission computer, and a commercial colour multi-function display generator. The first flight dates for the Block 50 series were as follows: F-16C (90-0801) flew on October 22, 1991, and the first F-16D (90-0834) flew on April 1, 1992. Both Block 52 aircraft followed the same year, the F-16C (90-0809) flying on October 22, and F-16D (90-0893) following on November 24.

Singapore AF F-16Ds Block 52s also feature the bulged spine originally developed for the Israeli Air Forces F-16D Block 30s. The USAF uses the following official air tasking order designations to distinguish the following F-16C and D models. Night/adverse weather-capable Block 40 and 42 are referred to as F-16CG and F-16DG and the SEAD-

capable Block 50 and 52 airframes as F-16CJ & F-16DJ.

The USAF fleet of around 650 Block 40/42/50/52s is undergoing a major upgrade known as the Common Configuration Implementation Program (CCIP), which involves extensive changes to the cockpit and avionics. This began in June 1998 and flight-testing is currently under way at Edwards AFB. In June 2001, the first eight kits arrived at the Ogden Air Logistics Center at Hill AFB, Utah, where the modification work will take place in several phases. The first phase will add a modular mission computer and colour cockpit displays to the Block 50/52 models, and was scheduled for completion by January 2002. The next phase, from March 2002, consists of a combined electronic interrogator/transponder, giving the

Above: Because of defence cutbacks in 1991, the 81st FS at Spangdahlem eventually became the sole F-4G squadron within the Wing. These were retired in 1993 when the unit re-equipped with the Fairchild A-10A Thunderbolt II, which it still operates. (Jelle Sjoerdsma collection)

Right: The 343rd TFW originally flew Fairchild A-10A Thunderbolt IIs and Cessna O-2As until 1986 when the O-2s were replaced by Rockwell OV-10 Broncos. The OV-10s served until they were retired during 1990, which left one unit, the 18th TFS, flying A-10s. In 1991, the unit converted to the F-16 to perform the Close Air Support (CAS) role alongside the A-10, which had been retained by the unit, which took on the 354th FW numberplate during 1993 and which continues to fly the F-16. (Lockheed Martin)

Right: Having flown the F-16 Block 40 for several years, the 347th FW became an Army co-operation wing as part of the USAF restructuring plans during 1994. Although the wing continued to fly the F-16, it gained units flying the Fairchild A-10 and Lockheed C-130. As a result the word 'Fighter' was dropped from the title. The 69th, 70th and 308th FS were all deactivated and the 307th FS took on the 69th FS numberplate. The wing lasted until further cutbacks were made in 2000; both the 68th and 69th FS disbanded and the F-16s were allocated to other units. This F-16D Block 40 carries the code 'MY' for Moody and the Air Combat Command (ACC) badge on the tail, plus the 69th FS name on the fin tip. (USAF – S/Sgt Mike Reinhardt)

aircraft autonomous BVR interception capability. This enables the alternate carriage of the advanced FLIR targeting pod in addition to the HARM Targeting System pod, giving full capability to deploy Maverick missiles and laser-guided bombs. The first aircraft with this capability is due for delivery by September 2002. During 2003, a Link 16 Multi-Function Information Distribution System, a new NATO standard data-link aimed at enhancing information exchange between all systems, will be added, along with a Joint Helmet-Mounted Cueing System (JHMCS), and an electronic horizontal situation indicator. Block 40/42 aircraft will undergo this conversion from 2005.

Upgrades like these will bring all these F-16 models to a common avionics standard similar to the F-16 MLU and to that of current and future production aircraft. Under current plans, the last of 650 aircraft is due to be completed and redelivered to the Air Force in 2009. Meanwhile, several export customers are looking at this upgrade for their own fleets.

In 1999, Israel announced its intention to order 50 F-16 Block 50I two-seaters, with the option of ordering another 60 airframes at a later date. Israel finally took the option of another 52 in June 2001, bringing its total to 102, though it remains to be seen whether it will order the last eight of the 60 options. The Block 50I aircraft will be powered by Pratt & Whitney F100-PW-229 engines and the aircraft's conformal fuel tanks and video data-link equipment will be produced by Israel Aircraft Industries (IAI). Elbit Systems will supply advanced avionics and a helmet-mounted display. The aircraft will feature new electronic warfare systems developed by another Israeli company, Elisra, and will carry weapons and sensors from Rafael. Deliveries of the first batch of aircraft are due to begin early in 2003.

138 FG. Oklahoma ANG

Top: Lockheed Martin fitted electro-luminescent exterior lighting strips to four F-16s in 1995 as part of a USAF tactics development and evaluation programme aimed at enhancing the aircraft's visibility during operational missions with friendly forces. A large number of the operational aircraft operated by the US forces are equipped with these lighting strips, apart from the F-16 fleet. No.88-0542 was the first aircraft to undergo these modifications and is seen at Fort Worth, prior to being redelivered to the 57th Wing at Nellis AFB. It served with the unit until August 8, 2000, when it collided with another F-16C and crashed into the Mormon mountains 50 miles (80km) from Nellis. The pilot ejected safely and the other aircraft managed to land safely, despite sustaining minor damage. (Lockheed Martin)

Upper centre: Oklahoma's ANG unit is the 125th FS, reporting to the 138th FW, flying from Tulsa International Airport. It converted to F-16 Block 42s after flying the LTV A-7D Corsair II. (USAF)

Lower centre: Singapore is the second customer to purchase F-16Ds with the large spine for extra avionics, the first customer being Israel. This is the first production aircraft undergoing a test flight out of Fort Worth in 1998. (Lockheed Martin)

Bottom: Most of the NATO member countries regularly participate in various exercises and squadron exchanges, which offer the opportunity to interact with different units and other air forces. This Greek AF F-16D took part in a squadron exchange with one of the Royal Air Force Jaguar Squadron's based at RAF Coltishall, Norfolk. (RAF)

Above: Two brand-new F-16C Block 50, seen parked outside at Fort Worth while awaiting collection and delivery to the USAF, the aircraft in the top photo was delivered to the 20th FW. The other aircraft entered service with the 52nd FW. (Both Lockheed Martin)

Greece ordered 50 F-16 Block 52+ on March 10, 2000, comprising 34 F-16C and 16 F-16D. These aircraft are essentially similar to the F-16I purchased by Israel, though they will not have the avionics specified by the Israelis. Greek aircraft will be equipped with the improved Northrop Grumman APG-68 (V) XM radar, will carry conformal fuel tanks, and will be powered by the Pratt & Whitney F100-PW-229. Deliveries are due to start in 2002 and continue until 2004. Greece also has options to buy an additional batch of ten aircraft.

When the United Arab Emirates receives the first of 80 F-16 Block 60s in 2004, it will be acquiring a new generation of F-16s, an aircraft capable of precision strike missions at night and in bad weather. This aircraft will have new systems developed by Northrop Grumman, including an Agile Beam Radar (ABR), internal FLIR and targeting systems (IFTS) and a new Integrated Electronic Warfare System (IEWS), plus the ability to carry conformal fuel tanks. A total of 55 of this variant will be single-seat and the remaining 25 will be two-seaters. The General Electric F110-GE-132, which can produce 144.6kN thrust, has been specifically developed to power the Block 60 airframe. Both the Israelis and the USAF have expressed interest in purchasing the Block 60. Lockheed Martin has given the current Block 50/52 export versions the model name Viper 2000. The Block 60 model has been given the designation Viper 2100.

Left: Production of the first F-16 Block 60 commenced during 2001, and this latest variant is due to make its first flight in late 2003. The majority of the changes are internal, although there are several external differences. The most obvious is the ability to carry Conformal Fuel Tanks (CFT), which allows the aircraft to be fitted with a larger choice of weapons on the wing pylons, normally reserved for drop tanks. Another change is the addition of a navigation sensor in the turret just in front of the cockpit, which is part of the integrated FLIR and targeting system developed by Northrop Grumman. (Lockheed Martin)

Left: Five F-16Cs from the 14th FS undergo routine maintenance between missions during Exercise Cope Thunder at Eielson AFB, Alaska, in July 1994. The unit is based at Misawa air base in Japan, and was assigned to the 432nd FW until the Wing gained the 35th FW numberplate in October 1994. Both the 13th and 14th FS flew the Block 15 model from 1984, converting to Block 30s in 1990 and subsequently to Block 50s in 1995. (KEY Archive)

Below: This AFRC F-16C from the 301st FW performs a tight turn on take-off, causing moist air vortices to stream off the fuselage. (USAF)

Below left: A Turkish AF F-16C Block 40 seen undergoing avionics modification and routine maintenance at Turkish Aerospace Industries (TAI) factory at Akinci, near Ankara. (KEY – Alan Warnes)

Right: Several F-16s from the 416th Flight Test Squadron (FTS), on the flightline at Edwards AFB, California. The nearest aircraft, a Block 40, has had part of the rear fuselage removed to allow the ground crew easy access to perform maintenance on the exhaust nozzle 'turkey feathers'. (KEY – Steve Fletcher)

Right: Most of the units with the USAF, and with the ANG and AFRC, have long histories and have often painted aircraft in special colour schemes to commemorate past events. The 174th FS of the Iowa ANG re-formed during 1946 and painted this aircraft in a spectacular gold scheme for its 50th anniversary in 1996. (Andy Marden)

Right: Another variation on the one-off colour scheme is the traditional 'Boss bird', an aircraft repainted with an appropriate serial number as the squadron commander's aircraft. The example shown here, 84-1286 was painted in 1985 for the 'Boss' of the 86th TFW. (Ian Black)

Below: An F-16D from 181 Filo performing aerodynamic braking while landing at RAF St Mawgan, Cornwall, in September 1997. It was one of a pair taking part in Exercise Ample Train. (KEY – Steve Fletcher)

Above: In 1994, the third production F-16 was used for the F-16 Enhanced Strategic (ES) trials, which formed the basis for what will eventually become the F-16 Block 60 for the United Arab Emirates Air Force. (Lockheed Martin)

Left: Over the years, the first three production F-16Cs for the USAF have undertaken a wide variety of trials. The second production aircraft, 83-1119, has gained the AIFF antenna normally found on either F-16ADF, or F-16MLU aircraft. In 1997, it took part in Lockheed Martin trials for 'paintless' aircraft, which involved applying a black adhesive pressure-sensitive film to most of the upper fuselage and wing surfaces. This aimed to save weight, cut costs and help prevent the environmental emissions produced when conventional paint is used. (Lockheed Martin)

Centre left: Another feature which is due to appear on future F-16s is the Pratt & Whitney Low Observable Axisymmetric Nozzle (LOAN). Trials of this nozzle, designed to reduce radar cross-section and infra-red signature emissions, took place in 1996. (Lockheed Martin)

Left: Two F-16Cs of the 8th Fighter Wing taxying out at Kunsan AB, Republic of Korea, for a station exercise in February 2001. Both aircraft are armed with AIM-9 Sidewinders and AIM-120 AMRAAM. (USAF/SSgt Jerry Morrison)

MITSUBISHI F-2 ⑤

Below: The first prototype of the Mitsubishi F-2 completed its maiden flight on October 7, 1995 – it is seen here during an early test flight wearing an interim serial number. After delivery to the Air Test and Development Wing (ATDW) at Gifu air base, this aircraft adopted the full Japanese Air Self Defence Force (JASDF) serial, 63-8501. The larger wing and bigger cockpit canopy are clearly visible in this view. Flight testing of the aircraft was completed during 2000.

The Mitsubishi F-2 is a development of the Lockheed Martin F-16, based on the 1980s Agile Falcon design concept, which was itself based on an F-16C Block 40 with a 25% larger wing. Designed as the next-generation close support fighter, it is currently entering squadron service with the Japanese Air Self Defence Force (JASDF), replacing the Mitsubishi F-1. The Japanese aircraft industry has a long history of producing license-built aircraft, including the North American F-86 which was followed by the Lockheed F-104 Starfighter, McDonnell Douglas F-4 Phantom II and the F-15 Eagle. However, for the next-generation Close Support Fighter it chose to develop the aircraft on its own, though still using an existing type as the basic design.

The basic design options were as follows: General Dynamics F-16, McDonnell Douglas F/A-18 and Panavia Tornado IDS, an indigenous aircraft design having already been abandoned. Mitsubishi Heavy Industries is undertaking final assembly at its Komaki South factory at Nagoya International Airport. The principal US sub-contractor is Lockheed Martin Aeronautics, which joined the project in 1996, producing the aft fuselage, wing leading-edge flaps and stores management systems. In addition it provides 80% of all left-hand wing boxes and various other avionics with related support equipment. Flight trials using the four prototypes were completed towards the end of 2000. The current order calls for procurement to run to 130 airframes: of these, 83 are F-2A and 47 are F-2B. The first deliveries of production aircraft were to the Provisional F-2 Hikotai (Squadron) and began on October 3, 2000, the unit gained its full complement of 18 aircraft by March 2001, enabling it to become 3 Hikotai. All the F-2s are scheduled to be delivered by 2010.

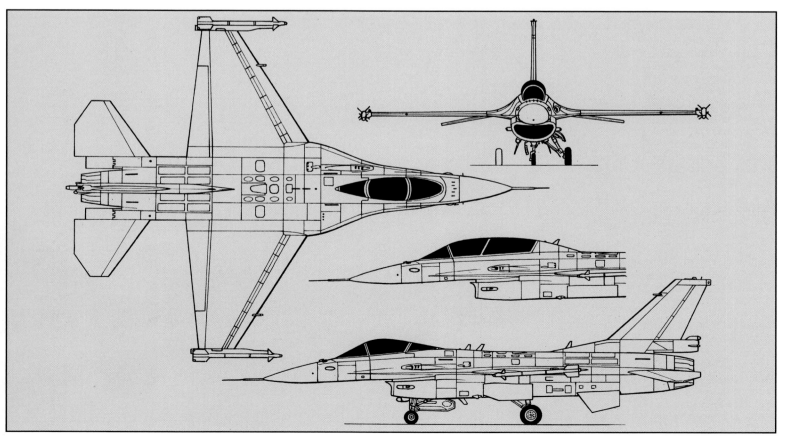

MITSUBISHI F-2 DATA

Length overall:	50ft 11in (15.52m)
Wingspan: (without wingtip missile launchers)	35ft 0in (10.80m)
Wingspan: (with wingtip missile launchers)	36ft 6in (11.125m)
Wing aspect ratio:	3.2
Height:	15ft 4 1/2in (5.09m)
Powerplant:	One General Electric F110-GE-129 turbofan
Increased performance engine (IPE) rated at	17,000lb st thrust (75.62kN) dry and 29,500lb st (131.22kN) with afterburner.
Empty weight:	18,917lb (8,581kg)
Max external load: (full internal fuel)	15,591lb (7,072kg)
Maximum internal fuel:	(JP-8) 7,162lb (3,208kg)
Maximum level speed:	above M2.0 at 40,000ft (12,200m)
Service ceiling:	50,000ft (15,240m)
Armament:	One JM61A1 20mm cannon in the port side wing/fuselage fairing with 511 rounds of ammunition, with up to 17,824lb (8,085kg) of disposable stores.

Top: Two of the four prototype F-2 airframes were built as two-seater aircraft. Of the 130 aircraft on order, 47 will be F-2Bs, and most of these will be assigned to Air Training Command at Matsushima. The remaining aircraft will be issued to three other operational units. (Tim Senior collection)

Above: Production F-2s have been painted in this two-tone blue colour scheme. The first of 130 production aircraft, F-2B 03-8106, is seen here being rolled out on September 25, 2000. (Yoshitomo Aoki)

Right: The first F-2A 03-8503 flew on October 12, making a further 22 test flights with the manufacturer and a further four test flights with the JASDF, prior to its final acceptance. (MHI via Yoshitomo Aoki)

Top: A close-up view of the canopy on a Belgian AF F-16AM, all USAF F-16C and D models, together with most NATO users, have a coat of gold film to dissipate radar energy. Also visible, just in front of the cockpit, are the aerials for the Hazeltine AN/APX-113 Identification Friend or Foe (IFF) interrogator/transponder. Below that is the slightly bulged fairing for the Radar Warning Receiver (RWR). (KEY – Alan Warnes)

Centre right: Current production F-16s are equipped with the upgraded AN/APG 68 radar replacing the earlier AN/APG-66. With the radome opened up for inspection, you get a good idea of the radar's compact size – illustrated by the example fitted inside this USAF Block 40 F-16D. An updated version of this radar, the AN/APG-68 (V) XM, became available for new production F-16s during early 2002, although it is also available as an upgrade for older aircraft. (Lockheed Martin)

Below: The IAI F-16B ACE demonstrator's original AN/APG-66 radar has been replaced with the IAI/ELTA EL/M2032 multi-mode fire control radar. (KEY – Alan Warnes)

Below right: Several customers purchased aircraft equipped with a searchlight to aid identification of unidentified aircraft. This is a Greek AF F-16C Block 30. (RAF)

The aircraft seen in most of the detail photographs in this chapter is an F-16AM of the Belgian AF. The pictures were taken at RAF Waddington while the aircraft was being prepared for its next sortie on the BAE Systems ACMI range in the North Sea. Also illustrated in this section are some of the other internal and external differences between this and other models of the F-16 family.

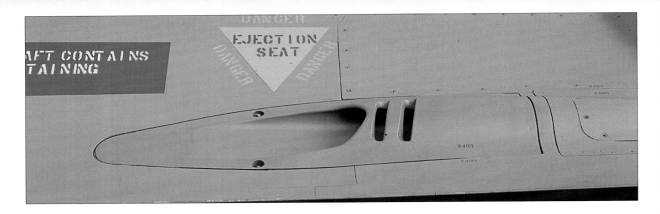

Left: A general view of the exhaust port for the M61 cannon fitted to the F-16 showing the protective layer of paint around it. The gun port on the F-16A differs from that on the F-16C in that it has more exhaust vents before and after. Also clearly visible are the large number of warning and escape details stencilled around the cockpit area. (KEY – Steve Fletcher)

Left: Belgian AF aircraft have this prominent antenna on the intake lip, it contains part of the Carapace ECM and threat warning system developed by Dassault electronic systems. (KEY – Steve Fletcher)

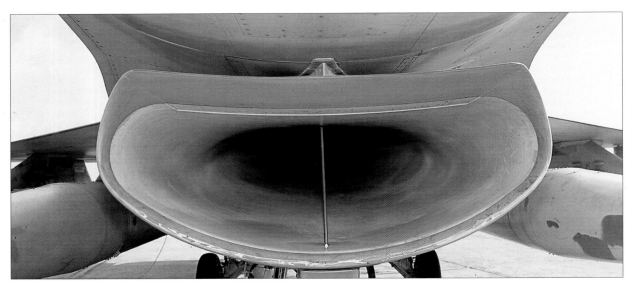

Left: All F-16s built up to Block 25 standard had the small intake fitted. (KEY – Steve Fletcher)

Below: The introduction of GE-powered aircraft from Block 30 onwards meant that a slightly larger intake was required. Aircraft with the larger inlets have gained the nickname 'Big Mouth'. (Jim Winchester)

Above left and above right: The F-16 nosewheel is located aft of the intake to prevent debris from being ingested into it. During take-off the nosewheel rotates 90 degrees and fits flush, horizontally within the intake ducting. Also visible in this photo are the landing lights fitted as standard to Block 40 aircraft onwards, and refitted to MLU aircraft during conversion. The nosewheel is fully steerable and is operated by depressing the rudder pedals. (KEY – Steve Fletcher)

Left and below: While the nosewheel retracts backwards, the main undercarriage retracts forwards into the wheel bays. Landing lights on the older model aircraft are attached to the mainwheel legs. Despite the sturdy design of the undercarriage, the aircraft is apparently tricky to land in crosswind conditions. (KEY – Steve Fletcher)

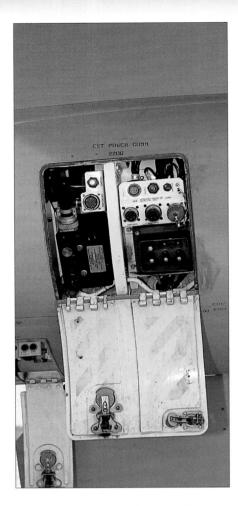

Above: While the aircraft is parked at dispersal, the groundcrew occasionally need to power up the aircraft systems when performing maintenance. To do this, they connect the generator up to the plug pictured lower right. (KEY – Steve Fletcher)

Above: All F-16s are equipped with an arrestor hook for emergency landings, and this is located in a semi-recessed section of the rear fuselage between and slightly aft of the ventral fins. (KEY – Steve Fletcher)

Below: Air-to-air refuelling is performed via the centrally-mounted refuelling receptacle located aft of the cockpit. This North Dakota ANG F-16B is being refuelled by a USAF Boeing KC-10 Extender. (USAF)

Below: The F-16 is refuelled on the ground with a single point high-pressure refuelling system, located above the port undercarriage door. (KEY – Steve Fletcher)

Above: F-16ADFs are easier to recognise as they have more avionics at the fin base. To accommodate them, a slightly more bulged fin base was added as part of the conversion process. (Robert F Dorr)

Top right: All the production models of the F-16C and D feature the extended fairing at the fin base, below the rudder, which houses more ECM equipment. (KEY – Duncan Cubitt)

Right: Early F-16s, including this Block 15 example, have the smaller ECM fairing fitted to the fin base, this is the small box-like structure, just above the engine exhaust. Some Israeli aircraft have a chaff/ flare dispenser 'scabbed' on to the front of the fin. (KEY – Duncan Cubitt)

Below: The brake parachute is housed in an extended tail-cone and was incorporated in Norwegian aircraft during construction – aircraft operated by Greece, Indonesia, Taiwan and Venezuela also have it fitted as standard. (KEY – Alan Warnes)

Below right: Belgian aircraft have subsequently been refitted with this tailcone, which contains part of the Carapace ECM system. Most of the remaining aircraft in the Netherlands have also had this added. (KEY – Steve Fletcher)

Top left: A close-up of the exhaust nozzle of a Pratt & Whitney F100-PW-220 engine, with the exhaust vanes fully open and the 'turkey feathers' in the closed position. These are slightly larger on aircraft powered by the General Electric F110-GE-100 series engine. (KEY – Steve Fletcher)

Centre left: Current production F-16s are powered by Pratt & Whitney's F100-PW-229 IPE engine, one of these is seen here during bench testing. (Pratt & Whitney)

Left: General Electric's F110-GE-129 is used to power all F-16 Block 30, 40 and 50 models, together with the Japanese development, the Mitsubishi F-2. (General Electric)

Right: This F-16AM of the Royal Netherlands AF will have a Pratt & Whitney F100-PW-220 re-installed after undergoing maintenance. (KEY – Steve Fletcher)

Left: The airbrakes on an F-16 are seen here in the fully open position, revealing holes cut into the structure to make the airbrakes as light as possible. The speed brakes can be pulled open manually while the aircraft is on the ground and there is no hydraulic power. In the distance, the ground crew prepares the aircraft for its next mission. (KEY – Steve Fletcher)

Right: The F-16 was designed from the beginning to be an easy aircraft to maintain, with readily accessible systems. F-16A J-197 is seen here during maintenance at Leeuwarden. (KEY – Steve Fletcher)

Below: Inside the maintenance hangar at Leeuwarden – with various panels removed for maintenance, this view gives a good indication of how complex a modern aircraft can be. (KEY – Steve Fletcher)

⑦ WEAPONS

F-16s can carry an impressive variety of weapons; for the air-to-air role these include the AIM-7 Sparrow, AIM-9 Sidewinder and AIM-120 AMRAAM. Later production F-16s have the ability to fight their way to and from the target at the same time as delivering ordnance. Air-to-ground weapons carried by F-16s include the Paveway family of laser-guided bombs which are delivered using either the Lockheed Martin LANTIRN pod or its downgraded Sharpshooter version. The Israeli AF uses the Rafael Litening pod with its own inventory of precision guided munitions. F-16s can also carry a wide selection of 'dumb' – but just as effective – iron bombs. Other precision-guided air-to-ground weapons include the AGM-65 Maverick, AGM-88 HARM, AGM-154 Joint Stand-Off Weapon (JSOW) and the GBU-29 Joint Direct Attack Munition (JDAM).

Above: One of the best-known air-to-air missiles carried by F-16s is the AIM-9 Sidewinder. This one is mounted on the wing tip launch rail of a 401st TFW F-16C formerly based at Torrejon in Spain. (KEY – Duncan Cubitt)

Below: The AIM-7F Sparrow was selected for carriage by US Air Force F-16ADFs: one is seen being launched by an F-16A from Edwards AFB. This F-16A has undergone various upgrades which almost bring it up to F-16C standard. (General Dynamics)

Right: A close-up of two AIM-9 Sidewinders carried on a Royal Netherlands AF F-16A. Up to six of these missiles can be carried, two on each wingtip station and two more on underwing pylons. Most of the nations that purchased F-16s bought the AiM-9P, L or M version of the Sidewinder. (KEY Archive)

Centre right: The AIM-120 AMRAAM is currently used by the USAF and some of the European air forces operating the F-16 Mid Life Update. The Belgian aircraft in this photo is also carrying an Air Combat Manoeuvring and Instrumentation (ACMI) pod and has just returned from a practice mission against Royal Navy Sea Harrier FA.2s. (KEY – Steve Fletcher)

Below: This early F-16C from the 39th FTS took part in early firing trials and other development work for the Advanced Short Range Air-to-Air Missile (ASRAAM), which is undergoing development for the Royal Air Force where it will replace the AIM-9.

Left: The Israeli company, Rafael, has developed and refined a family of air-to-air missiles over the last 30 years. Israeli AF F-16s initially carried the Rafael Shafrir II and currently use two versions of the Rafael Python. The Python III was introduced in 1991, and the Python IV followed in 1997. Two Python IVs are seen mounted on an Israeli AF F-16C. (Rafael)

Left: Israeli F-16s will eventually be able to carry the Rafael Derby, an advanced BVR Air-to-Air Missile. It can be used for short-range aerial engagements, though at the time of writing it had not been test-fired from an F-16. The manufacturer has wasted no time in showing it to the aviation industry and the public – one missile is seen here mounted on the wingtip pylon of the upgraded F-16ACE at the Paris Airshow in June 2001. (KEY – Alan Warnes)

Left: The AGM-88 High Speed Anti-Radiation Missile (HARM) is used in the SEAD role, in conjunction with the HARM Targeting System pod mounted on the intake chin which locates the energy from radar emissions. One is seen here being fired from an F-16C of the 14th Fighter Squadron based at Misawa AB, Japan. F-16s have also fired the earlier AGM-45 Shrike anti-radiation missile, though this has now been retired from service.

Left: The F-16 has been cleared to fire several versions of the AGM-65 Maverick family of air-to-surface missiles. These include the A model, which has an Electro Optical (EO) television seeker. The AGM-65B is similar, although it has Scenery Magnification (Scene Mag) capability, enabling it to be locked on to a target from twice the range. Both the D and G models have Imaging Infra-Red (IIR) capability, which can be used at night and in hazy/smoky conditions. A pair of AGM-65Gs are pictured being carried by an F-16C of the 56th FW. (USAF)

Right: Norway is the only F-16 operator to use the A-S Kongsberg Penguin III air-to-surface anti-shipping missile, four of which are shown on handling trolleys in front of a 332 Skvadron F-16A. Korean and Egyptian F-16s carry the AGM-84 Harpoon for the anti-shipping mission. (KEY Archive)

Centre right: During the 1980s, the French firm Aérospatiale used this unmarked F-16 to undertake firing trials of the AS 30 air-to-surface missile. These tests were made in conjunction with the Thompson CSF ATLIS targeting pod that is visible on the starboard intake chin station. (CEV)

Below: Israel has cleared the Rafael Popeye, a rocket-powered stand-off missile, for use on its F-16s, and it has now been integrated for use with USAF F-16s as the AGM-142A Have Nap. A slightly lighter version, known as the Popeye II/AGM-142B Have Lite, is also currently in service with the Israeli AF, and has been exported to Korea and Turkey.

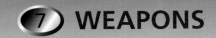

Left: Modern warfare still has a place for traditional 'dumb' bombs, which are usually employed in bombing enemy troop concentrations in order to drain morale and effect a speedy conclusion to the conflict. A 419th Fighter Wing F-16C is pictured just after releasing a single 500lb Mk 82 bomb over the Utah Test and Training Range. (USAF/SSgt Gary R Coppage)

Centre left: An F-16A from the now disbanded 429th TFS, once part of the 474th TFW based at Nellis AFB, drops a stick of four 2,000lb (907kg), Mk 84 Low Drag General Purpose (LDGP) bombs. These are the largest dumb bombs in the USAF inventory that can be carried by fighters: the combination was used during the later stages of Operation Desert Storm. (Robert F Dorr collection)

Bottom left: The Paveway family of Precision Guided Munitions (PGM) has improved considerably since introduced during the South East Asia conflict in the 1970s. This 500lb Mk 82 General Purpose Bomb has been turned into a Paveway II by simply adding the laser designator to the front and movable fins to the rear: the bomb is then given the designation GBU-12 (GBU for Glide Bomb Unit). This one has just been released from a 388th FW F-16C. (Raytheon)

Below: Another method of delivering bombs is shown in this view of a Royal Netherlands AF F-16B, which has just dropped a pair of 2,000lb (907kg) Mk 84 'ballute' parachute retarded bombs. These are usually employed in low-level attacks – the parachute deploys and slows the bomb down, allowing the aircraft dropping it to escape the blast and debris. (Key Archive)

Above: The F-16C Block 50s operated by the 20th FW at Shaw AFB became the first USAF wing and the first F-16 unit to operate some of the next generation of air-to-ground weapons. Among these is the AGM-154A Joint Stand-Off Weapon (JSOW), two of which can be carried on the wing pylons. Other weapons introduced included the GBU-31 Joint Direct Attack Munition (JDAM), and the CBU-103/104/105 versions of the Wind-Corrected Munitions Dispenser. All these weapons have inertial guidance systems, and JSOW and JDAM are equipped with a Global Positioning System (GPS). (USAF – T/Sgt Cary Humphries)

Centre right: The USAF has tested several other weapons for future use with USAF F-16 units, including the Joint Air-to-Surface Stand-off Missile (JASSM), seen here being released from a 416th FTS F-16D. (Lockheed Martin)

Right: Another weapon destined for American and some international F-16 users, is the Autonomous Free-Flight Dispenser System (AFDS), which has been developed in co-operation with EADS/DASA of Germany. AFDS is a free-fall glide dispenser fitted with two stub wings. Testing has been carried out at Eglin AFB, though this weapon has not currently been ordered by any F-16 operator. (Tim Senior collection)

Top left: Among the lesser-known roles of the USAF F-16s is Forward Air Control - Airborne (FACA), and the 31st FW, based at Aviano AB in northern Italy, is one of the units most experienced in this. F-16s performing this mission carry the LAU-68 rocket pod, which can be loaded with white phosphorous or smoke markers to mark targets for other incoming attacking aircraft. (KEY – Alan Warnes)

Top right: Most countries operating F-16s initially used them solely for the air defence mission. Although some have already adopted a multi-role mission, others are still changing over to this role. The ability to successfully drop laser-guided bombs and other smart weapons requires accurate designation, either by ground-based means, such as special forces troops with hand-held designators, or by choosing one of the podded systems available. The most widely-used pod is the Lockheed Martin Low Altitude Navigation and Targeting Infra-Red for Night (LANTIRN), seen here in its targeting pod form on a Royal Netherlands AF F-16A. (KEY – Archive)

Left: The other LANTIRN pod is used for low-altitude navigation. Both pods are seen attached to the intake of this F-16C based at Edwards AFB. (KEY Archive)

Right: The Royal Netherlands AF was initially the only customer to use its F-16s in the reconnaissance role, continuing to operate with the Delft Orpheus pod which had been in use since the early 1970s. Although General Dynamics planned a recce version of the F-16, this project remained largely dormant until the early 1990s. However, due to shrinking defence budgets, several countries retired dedicated reconnaissance aircraft, forcing them to re-equip F-16s for this role. Denmark became the first country to do this, initially using the Red Baron pod, which is seen here on the centreline of an F-16 containing systems from Saab Drakens. (Tim Senior)

Right: After the USAF retired its McDonnell Douglas RF-4C Phantoms, it undertook trials with several systems. One was dubbed 'the Richmond recce pod' after Richmond International Airport where the Virginian ANG is based. (Lockheed Martin)

Lower right: Elta of Israel has developed its own reconnaissance system and has fitted Synthetic Aperture Radar (SAR) into a modified fuel tank. This system carries the designation EL/M-2060P, and is mounted to the centreline of the aircraft. This cut-away mock-up was displayed at the Paris airshow in June 2001. (KEY – Malcolm English)

Far left: Two other targeting pods are used by F-16 operators, one is the Rafael Litening, seen here attached to the Israel Aircraft Industries-developed F-16ACE. (KEY – Alan Warnes)

Left: Thompson CSF developed the ATLIS pod, which has been purchased by the Pakistani and Thai Air Forces. (KEY – John Barker)

Right: Four countries – Belgium, Denmark, the Netherlands, and the USA (via an eventual five wings of the USAF ANG) – will undertake reconnaissance operations with the Modular Reconnaissance Pod built by the Danish company, TERMA Industries. (Tim Senior)

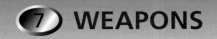

Above: Per Udsen Industries of Denmark has developed several systems enabling aircraft to better defend themselves while undertaking air-to-ground missions. This is mainly due to new and more complex Surface-to-Air Missiles (SAMs). The Danish AF gave the company the task of modifying standard aircraft pylons to incorporate an additional chaff dispenser and associated electronics. It developed the Pylon Integrated Dispenser System (PIDS) which has three AN/ALE-40 chaff and flare dispensers built in. This system is used by the air forces of Belgium, Denmark, and the Netherlands and by the USAF's ANG and AFRC. (KEY – Alan Warnes)

Centre left: An enhanced and further updated version of PIDS, known as PIDS+, has been developed in conjunction with Denmark, the Netherlands and Norway. Earlier PIDS can be brought up to this standard very quickly, and both can be fitted with Electronic Counter-measures (ECM) systems such as the Northrop Grumman AN/ALQ-162 jammer. (KEY – Alan Warnes)

Left: The AN/ALQ-131 is used by most of the European countries operating the F-16. The picture shows one mounted beneath a Belgian AF F-16AM. (KEY – Steve Fletcher)

The list of operators presented here include all the current countries, wings and units flying the F-16. Squadron nick-names and fin tip colours, have been included where they are known. Also included are complete serial allocations and aircraft write-offs complete with date and serials where known. AFM regularly features updates on unit changes and aircraft losses.

Bahrain AF 1st Fighter Squadron

Belgian AF No1 Fighter Squadron

BAHRAIN			
Bahrain Amiri Air Force			
1st Fighter Squadron Shaikh Isa	F-16C/D Block 40		
2nd Fighter Squadron Shaikh Isa	F-16C/D Block 40		
F-16C Block 40			
101	90-0028	111	90-0033
103	90-0029	113	90-0034
105	90-0030	115	90-0035
107	90-0031	201 to 210	98-2012
109	90-0032		to 98-2021
F-16D Block 40			
150	90-0036	154	90-0038
152	90-0037	156	90-0039

CURRENT AND FUTURE F-16 OPERATORS

Current Operators

Bahrain	Pakistan
Belgium	Portugal
Denmark	Singapore
Egypt	South Korea
Greece	Taiwan
Indonesia	Thailand
Israel	Turkey
Jordan	United States of
The Netherlands	America
Norway	Venezuela

Future Operators

Chile	Oman
Italy	United Arab Emirates

Above: After purchasing a mixed batch of 12 Block 40 F-16C/Ds during 1990, the Bahrain Amiri AF purchased a second batch of ten F-16Cs. The first aircraft of this batch is seen during a pre-delivery test flight, while still wearing the last three digits from its Foreign Military Serial (FMS), these are standard US fiscal year serial numbers assigned to all export F-16s. (Lockheed Martin)

Below: The Belgian AF painted F-16A FA-67 in this special colour scheme during 1998, to celebrate the 20th anniversary of the F-16 entering service with the Belgian forces. The first aircraft, F-16B, FB-01 made its first flight in December 1978. (KEY – Alan Warnes)

BELGIUM

**Belgian Air Force
(Force Aérienne Belge/ Belgische Luchtmacht)**

2nd Tactische Wing, Florennes

1 Smaldeel	F-16AM/BM
350 Smaldeel	F-16AM/BM

10th Tactische Wing, Kleine Brogel

31 Smaldeel	F-16AM/BM
349 Smaldeel	F-16AM/BM
Operational Conversion Unit	F-16AM/BM

F-16A

Block 01	FA-01 to FA-17	78-0116 to 78-0132
Block 05	FA-18 to FA-25	78-0133 to 78-0140
Block 10	FA-26 to FA-46	78-0141 to 78-0161
	FA-47 to FA-55	80-3538 to 80-3546
Block 15	FA-56 to FA-96	80-3547 to 80-3587
	FA-97 to FA-101	86-0073 to 86-0077
	FA-102 to FA-112	87-0046 to 87-0056
	FA-113 to FA-122	88-0038 to 88-0047
	FA-123 to FA-133	89-0001 to 89-0011
	FA-134 to FA-136	90-0025 to 90-0027

F-16B

Block 01	FB-01 to FB-06	78-0162 to 78-0167
Block 05	FB-07 to FB-10	78-0168 to 78-0171
Block 10	FB-11 to FB-12	78-0172 to 78-0173
Block 15	FB-13 to FB-20	80-3588 to 80-3595
	FB-21	87-0001
	FB-22 to FB-23	88-0048 to 88-0049
	FB-24	89-0012

Losses

F-16A	
FA-06 w/o 2.9.85	FA-54 w/o 18.10.89
FA-07 w/o 10.11.83	FA-59 w/o 21.9.83
FA-08 w/o 28.7.80	FA-62 w/o 17.11.88
FA-11 w/o 12.3.81	FA-63 w/o 15.9.87
FA-12 w/o 18.10.89	FA-64 w/o 7.9.93
FA-13 w/o 10.5.83	FA-79 w/o 30.6.86
FA-14 w/o 19.1.82	FA-80 w/o 29.4.97
FA-15 w/o 17.11.88	FA-85 w/o 25.10.89
FA-24 w/o 29.4.85	FA-96 w/o 8.1.02
FA-29 w/o 22.10.81	FA-105 w/o 5.9.89
FA-33 w/o 19.8.86	FA-113 w/o 12.5.95
FA-35 w/o 19.1.82	
FA-39 w/o 23.3.99	**F-16B**
FA-41 w/o 10.11.83	FB-06 w/o 13.7.89
FA-42 w/o 9.10.86	FB-11 w/o 23.6.93
FA-52 w/o 19.9.87	FB-13 w/o 9.1.92
	FB-16 w/o 19.9.84

Left: An F-16AM takes off for another mission from RAF Waddington, the aircraft is carrying AIM-9 Sidewinders and AIM-120 AMRAAMs. Defence cuts announced during 2001, left the BAF with just four fighter squadrons. No 2 Squadron merged with No 350 Squadron at Florennes during April 2001 to form a larger unit, while No 23 Squadron at Kleine Brogel followed during early 2002, passing its aircraft to the OCU. (KEY – Steve Fletcher)

Belgian AF No 2 Fighter Squadron

Belgian AF No 31 Fighter Squadron

Belgian AF No 349 Fighter Squadron

Belgian AF No 350 Fighter Squadron

Left: Several countries within NATO make extensive use of the BAE Systems' North Sea Range (NSR) which is an Air Combat Manoeuvring Instrumentation (ACMI) range situated 70 miles (113km) out to sea. Belgian AF F-16s regularly visit this facility, often deploying several different squadrons at a time to the main operating base at RAF Waddington, Lincolnshire. Each unit usually performs about three missions per day, here F-16BM FB-20 is seen taxying out for another sortie during March 2001. The Air Instrumentation Sub-system (AIS) pod underneath its wing records all the data from each mission and can be played back during the mission de-brief. (KEY – Steve Fletcher)

Left: F-16A FA-116 was painted in this special colour scheme during 2001, to celebrate both the 50th anniversary of 31 Squadron and the 40th anniversary of the NATO Tiger association. Each year, all the NATO squadrons that feature either a tiger or another big cats in the squadron badge, get together to discuss tactics. By flying with – and against – each other they are able to establish closer operational relationships. (KEY – Steve Fletcher)

DENMARK

Royal Danish Air Force (Flyvevåbnet)
Eskadrille 726 Aalborg   F-16AM/BM
Eskadrille 727 Skrystrup   F-16AM/BM
Eskadrille 730 Skrystrup   F-16AM/BM

F-16A

Block 01	E-174 to E-176	78-0174 to 78-0176
Block 05	E-177 to E-178	78-0177 to 78-0188
Block 10	E-189 to E-203	78-0189 to 78-0203
Block 15	E-596 to E-611	80-3596 to 78-3611
	E-004 to E-008	87-0004 to 87-0008
	E-016 to E-018	88-0016 to 88-0018

F-16B

Block 01	ET-204 to ET-205	78-0204 to 78-0205
Block 05	ET-206 to ET-208	78-0206 to 78-0208
Block 10	ET209 to ET-211	78-0209 to 78-0211
Block 15	ET-612 to ET-615	80-3612 to 80-3615
	ET-197 to ET-199	86-0197 to 86-0199
	ET-022	87-0022

Ex USAF aircraft

First batch delivered July 7, 1994		Second Batch delivered March 25, 1997	
E-024	82-1024	E-011	82-1011
E-107	83-1107	E-070	83-1070
E-075	83-1075	E074	83-1074
		ET-626	80-0626

Losses

F-16A	
E-175 w/o 5.4.83	E-201 w/o 7.2.87
E-178 w/o 2.4.01	
E-179 w/o 1.4.85	**F-16B**
E-185 w/o 10.12.87	ET-205 w/o 11.12.96
E-186 w/o 1.4.85	ET-209 w/o 19.6.84
	ET-211 w/o 19.6.84

Danish AF 726 Squadron

Danish ADF 727 Squadron

Danish AF 730 Squadron

Top: Special markings on Danish F-16s are rare – even the squadron badges are confined to a small area either on the intake or tail. Occasionally, however, some do appear with 'zaps' painted on them; however, the significance of the Homer Simpson badge on the tail of this F-16BM from Eskadrille 726 is unknown. (KEY – Steve Fletcher)

Centre: Four Danish squadrons operated F-16s until January 8, 2001, when 723 Squadron at Aalborg disband-

ed during a ceremony to commemorate its 50th anniversary. (KEY – Steve Fletcher)

Above: This Danish AF F-16A is carrying two different versions of inert AIM-9 Sidewinders, both of which are used only for training purposes. On the port wingtip it is carrying an AIM-9J, while it has an AIM-9L on the starboard. (Ian Black)

EGYPT		
Egyptian Air Force		
(Al Quwwatal Jawwiya il Misriya)		
232nd Fighter Regiment	**An Shas AB**	
72nd Fighter Squadron	F-16A/B Block 15	
74th Fighter Squadron	F-16A/B Block 15	
242nd Fighter Regiment	**Beni Suef**	
68th Fighter Squadron	F-16C/D Block 32	
70th Fighter Squadron	F-16C/D Block 32	
262nd Fighter Regiment	**Abu Suwayr**	
60th Fighter Squadron	F-16C/D Block 40	
64th Fighter Squadron	F-16C/D Block 40	
272nd Fighter Regiment	**Genacklis**	
75th Fighter Squadron	F-16C/D Block 40	
77th Fighter Squadron	F-16C/D Block 40	
F-16A		
Block 15	9301 to 9305	80-0639 to 80-0643
	9306 to 9324	81-0643 to 81-0661
	9325 to 9334	82-1056 to 82-1065
F-16B		
Block 15	9201 to 9205	80-0644 to 80-0648
	9206	81-0662
	9207	81-0883
	9208	82-1043
F-16C		
Block 32	9501 to 9508	84-1332 to 84-1339
	9509 to 9534	85-1518 to 85-1543
Block 40	9901 to 9902	89-0278 to 89-0279
	9903 to 9934	90-0899 to 90-0930
	9935	90-0953
	9951 to 9978	93-0485 to 93-0512
	9979 to 9984	93-0525 to 93-0530
	0086 to 0106	96-0086 to 96-0106
		99-0105 to 99-0116
F-16D		
Block 32	9401 to 9406	84-1340 to 84-1345
Block 40	9801 to 9807	90-0931 to 90-0937
	9808 to 9812	90-0954 to 90-0958
	9851 to 9862	93-0513 to 93-0524
		99-0117 to 99-0128

EGYPT		
Losses		
F-16A	9332 w/o 3.8.92	9917 w/o 4.10.94
9311 w/o 6.11.90		9928 w/o 9.9.93
9312 w/o 2.10 91	**F-16B**	9935 w/o 7.4.97
9313 w/o 6.11.90	9204 w/o 20.1.83	
9316 w/o 21.5.87		**F-16D**
9320 w/o 3.8.92	**F-16C**	9807 w/o 7.4.97
9326 w/o 12.7.93	9520 w/o 10.5.94	9852 w/o 14.7.94
9327 w/o 15.3.95	9521 w/o 23.5.95	w/o 29.12.98

Top and above: Most of the combat aircraft in the Egyptian AF wear these high-visibility orange and black markings to aid identification over the harsh desert environment, and they also help to avoid mis-identification with other air forces (such as Israel) that operate the same type of aircraft. (Lockheed Martin)

Left: Delivery of the Peace Vector V aircraft for Egypt began during 1999 – 0086 is the first production air-craft from this batch, and is seen on a pre-delivery test flight. (Lockheed Martin)

Egyptian AF 68th Fighter
Squadron

Egyptian AF 68th Fighter
Squadron

Egyptian AF 70th Fighter
Squadron

Egyptian AF 262 Fighter
Regiment

Greek AF 330 Fighter
Squadron

GREECE			
Hellenic Air Force (Polemikí Aeroporía)			
	F-16C		
	Block 30	110 to 143	88-0110 to 88-0143
110 Pteriga Mahis Larissa	Block 50	045 to 076	93-1045 to 93-1076
346 Mira Dioxis Vomvardismou — F-16C/D Block 30			
	F-16D		
111 Pteriga Mahis Nea Ankkhialos	Block 30	144 to 149	88-0144 to 88-0149
330 Mira Dioxis Vomvardismou — F-16C/D Block 30	Block 50	077 to 084	93-1077 to 93-1084
341 Mira Dioxis Vomvardismou — F-16C/D Block 50			
347 Mira Dioxis Vomvardismou — F-16C/D Block 50	**Losses**		
F-16 OCU (Sminos	**F-16C**		135 w/o 15.7.93
Metekpedefsisston Tipo) — F-16C/D Block 30/50	123 w/o 13.11.00		137 w/o 26.11.92
	131 w/o 23.9.97		142 w/o 13.11.95

Above: Greece has now purchased three batches of F-16s. The first order placed during the late 1980s was for 40 Block 30 aircraft consisting of 34 F-16C and six F-16Ds. With the first batch well established in service, a second order was placed in 1993 for another 40, although these were for Block 50 models, comprising 32 F-16Cs and the remainder F-16Ds. This F-16C was photographed while landing at RAF St Mawgan in Cornwall while participating in Exercise Ample Train during September 1997. (KEY – Steve Fletcher)

Below: This is the second production F-16 Block 50 photographed before being delivered in 1997. Greece signed an order for 50 F-16s Block 50+ during March 2000 – originally it wanted 34 F-16Cs and 16 F-16Ds. However, during September 2001, the Greek Government decided to order ten more aircraft consisting of six additional single-seat and four two-seat aircraft. (Lockheed Martin)

INDONESIA

Indonesian Air Force
(Tentara Nasional Indonesia-Angkatan Udara)

Koopsali 2
Skwadron Udara 3

Ishwayudi
F-16A/B Block 15 OCU

F-16A
Block 15 TS-1605 to TS1612   87-0713 to 87-0720

F-16B
Block 15 TS-1601 to TS-1604   87-0721 to 87-0724

Losses
F-16A
TS-1607 w/o 11.3.97

F-16B
TS-1604 w/o 15.6.92

Indonesian 3rd Fighter
Squadron

ISRAEL

Israeli Air Force Heyl Ha'Avir
(Israeli Defence Force/Air Force)

Kanaf 1	Ramat David
Tayeset 109 *Valley*	Barak & Brakeet
Tayeset 110 *Knights of the North*	Barak & Brakeet
Tayeset 117 *First Jet*	Barak & Brakeet

Kanaf 4	Hatzor
Tayeset 101 *First Fighter*	Barak & Brakeet
Tayeset 105 *Scorpions*	Barak & Brakeet
Tayeset 144 *Guardians of the Arav*	Netz
Tayeset 601 IDF/AF RDT&E Unit	Barak & Brakeet

Kanaf 25	Ramon
Tayeset 140 *Golden Eagle*	Netz
Tayeset 147	Netz
Tayeset 253 *Neguev*	Netz

Kanaf 28	Nevatim
Tayeset 104	Netz
Tayeset 115 *Flying Dragon*	Netz
Tayeset 116 *Flying Wing*	Netz

F-16A

Block 01	78-0012	ex USAF
	78-0014	ex USAF
	78-0018	ex USAF
Block 05	78-0308 to 78-0325	
	79-0288	ex USAF
Block 10	78-0326 to 78-0354	
	79-0289	ex USAF
	79-0291 to 79-0293	
	79-0295	ex USAF
	79-0297	ex USAF
	79-0299	ex USAF
	79-0302	ex USAF
	79-0304 to 79-0305	ex USAF
	79-0319 to 79-0321	ex USAF
	79-0325	ex USAF
	79-0328	ex USAF
	79-0333	ex USAF
	79-0339	ex USAF
	79-0347	ex USAF
	79-0356	ex USAF
	79-0358	ex USAF
	79-0361	ex USAF
	79-0369	ex USAF
	79-0377	ex USAF
	80-0491	ex USAF
	80-0501 to 80-0503	ex USAF
	80-0514	ex USAF
	80-0516 to 80-0517	ex USAF
	80-0532	ex USAF
	80-0534	ex USAF
	80-0649 to 80-0668	

F-16B

Block 01	78-0086	ex USAF
	78-0095	ex USAF
Block 05	78-0106	ex USAF
	78-0108 to 78-0109	ex USAF
	78-0111	ex USAF
	78-0114 to 78-0115	ex USAF
	78-0355 to 78-0362	
	78-0410	ex USAF
Block 10	78-0423 to 78-0425	ex USAF
	80-0624	ex USAF
	80-0632	ex USAF

F-16C

Block 30	86-1598 to 86-1612	
	87-1661 to 87-1693	
	88-1709 to 88-1711	
Block 40	89-0277	
	90-0850 to 90-0874	
	91-0486 to 01-0489	

F-16D

Block 30	87-1694 to 87-1708	
	88-1712 to 88-1720	
Block 40	90-0875 to 90-0898	
	91-0490 to 91-0495	

Losses

121 w/o 5.10.87	??? w/o 1.8.00
222 w/o 20.1.81	003 w/o 8.10.86
225 w/o 7.12.86	008 w/o 29.6.81
227 w/o 28.8 83	015 w/o 18.12.88
237 w/o 2.2.00	??? w/o 7.9.97
240 w/o 10.4.86	??? w/o 1.00
257 w/o 20.11.81	368 w/o 9.8.98
266 w/o 20.1.82	077 w/o 23.3.00
269 w/o 17.9.95	606 w/o 18.7.95
276 w/o 20.1.82	621 w/o 5.10.94
277 w/o 2.7.86	660 w/o 18.7.95
290 w/o 17.1.95	??? w/o 29.3.99

Top: Two F-16As seen flying in formation over sparse Indonesian countryside. Due to the situation in East Timor, various governments are still imposing sanctions on the sales of weapons to Indonesia and this has affected plans to acquire a second batch of F-16s. The ten remaining aircraft were due to go through the Falcon-up avionics upgrade, but the country's financial crisis in 1997, combined with various other delays, has caused these plans to be put on hold for the foreseeable future. (Hendro Subroto)

Above: F-16A Netz 233 photographed near the Lebanese border during 1992. (via Shlomo Aloni)

Right: Two F-16Bs from the *'Golden Eagle'* Squadron await their turn to refuel, while another F-16B from the 'Negev' Squadron takes on fuel from a Boeing 707 Re'em (Ram). (via Shlomo Aloni)

Israeli *Golden Eagle* Squadron

Right: An Italian AF AMX leads a pair of *'Negev'* Squadron F-16Bs during a deployment to Italy in September 1999. (Via Shlomo Aloni)

Israeli *Negev* Squadron

Israeli *Scorpions* Squadron

Right: Fifty ex-USAF F-16A/Bs were transferred to the Israeli AF during 1994, and these were used to form the *'Phoenix'* Squadron. Shortly after they arrived in Israel most of the aircraft went through a modification programme to bring them up to a similar standard. This included repainting them into the three-tone desert camouflage scheme. (Shlomo Aloni)

Below: Lockheed Martin built the first 12 Block 52 F-16Cs for the Republic of Korea AF (RoKAF) – with deliveries starting in 1994. All subsequent deliveries, including an additional 68 F-16Cs and 40 F-16Ds, were licence-built by Samsung at Sachon in South Korea. (Lockheed Martin)

Bottom: South Korea placed an order for a further 20 Block 52s during 2000 – 15 of these will be F-16Cs, with the remaining five being F-16Ds. (Katsuhiko Tokunaga)

JORDAN

Jordanian Air Force
(Al Quwwat al Jawwiya al Malakiya al Urduniya)

No 2 Squadron	Azraq	F-16A/B ADF

F-16A Block 15ADF		229	81-0672
220	80-0544	230	81-0689
221	80-0546	231	81-0714
222	80-0547		
223	80-0555	**F-16B Block 15ADF**	
224	80-0582	232	82-1028
225	80-0585	233	82-1030
226	80-0590	234	82-1044
227	80-0592	235	82-1048
228	80-0618		

Losses	
F-16B	w/o 24.2.99

REPUBLIC OF KOREA

Republic of Korea Air Force
(Han-Guk Kong Goon)

19th Tactical Fighter Wing	Chungwon
155th Tactical Fighter Squadron	F-16C/D Block 52
159th Tactical Fighter Squadron	F-16C/D Block 52
161st Tactical Fighter Squadron	F-16C/D Block 32
162nd Tactical Fighter Squadron	F-16C/D Block 32

20th Tactical Fighter Wing	Sosan
120th Tactical Fighter Squadron	F-16C/D Block 52
123rd Tactical Fighter Squadron	F-16C/D Block 52

F-16C	
Block 30	86-1598 to 86-1612
	87-1661 to 87-1693
	88-1709 to 88-1711
Block 40	89-0277
	90-0850 to 90-0874
	91-0486 to 91-0489

F-16D	
Block 30	87-1694 to 87-1708
	88-1712 to 88-1720
Block 40	90-0875 to 90-0898
	91-0490 to 91-0495

**Republic of Korea AF
20th Fighter Wing**

**Royal Netherlands AF
306 Squadron**

**Royal Netherlands AF
311 Squadron**

REPUBLIC OF KOREA (continued)

F-16C

Block 32	85-574 to 85-583	85-1574 to 85-1583
	86-586 to 86-597	86-1586 to 86-1597
	87-653 to 87-660	87-1653 to 87-1660
Block 52	92-001 to 92-028	92-4001 to 92-4028
	93-049 to 93-100	93-4049 to 93-4100

F-16D

Block 32	84-370 to 84-373	84-1370 to 84-1373
	85-584 to 85-585	85-1584 to 85-1585
	90-938 to 90-941	90-0938 to 90-0941
Block 52	92-029 to 92-048	92-4029 to 92-4048
	93-101 to 93-120	93-4101 to 93-4120

Losses

F-16C	F-16D
87-1655 w/o 8.4.93	w/o 7.6.01
	w/o 6.8.97
	w/o 18.9.97

THE NETHERLANDS

**Royal Netherlands Air Force
(Koninklijke Luchtmacht)**

306 Squadron	Volkel	F-16AM/BM
311 Squadron	Volkel	F-16AM/BM
312 Squadron	Volkel	F-16AM/BM
Testgroep	Volkel	F-16AM/BM
313 Squadron	Twenthe	F-16AM/BM
315 Squadron	Twenthe	F-16AM/BM
322 Squadron	Leeuwarden	F-16AM/BM
323 Squadron	Leeuwarden	F-16AM/BM

THE NETHERLANDS (continued)

F-16A

Block 01	J-212 to J-223	78-0212 to 78-0223
Block 05	J-224 to J-237	78-0224 to 78-0237
Block 10	J-238 to J-257	78-0238 to 78-0257
Block 15	J-258	78-0258
	J-616 to J-648	80-3616 to 80-3648
	J-864 to J-881	81-0864 to 81-0881
	J-192 to J-207	83-1192 to 83-1207
	J-358 to J-367	84-1358 to 84-1367
	J-135 to J-146	85-0135 to 85-0146
	J-054 to J-063	86-0054 to 86-0063
	J-508 to J-516	87-0508 to 87-0516
	J-710	87-0710
	J-001 to J-012	88-0001 to 88-0012
	J-013 to J-021	88-0013 to 88-0021

F-16B

Block 01	J-259 to J-264	78-0259 to 78-0264
Block 05	J-265 to J-266	78-0265 to 78-0266
Block 10	J-267 to J-271	78-0267 to 78-0271
Block 15	J-649 to J-657	80-3649 to 80-3657
	J-882	81-0882
	J-884 to J-885	81-0884 to 81-0885
	J-208 to J-211	83-1208 to 83-1211
	J-368 to J-369	84-1368 to 84-1369
	J-064 to J-065	86-0064 to 86-0065
	J-066 to J-068	87-0066 to 87-0068

Losses

F-16A

J-007 w/o 10.1.92	J-358 w/o 10.5.90
J-012 w/o 10.1.96	J-359 w/o 24.9.92
J-054 w/o 11.2.92	J-361 w/o 23.9.99
J-056 w/o 19.4.89	J-618 w/o 26.5.92
J-059 w/o 22.12.99	J-621 w/o 3.6.85
J-140 w/o 21.5.98	J-625 w/o 4.6.88
J-195 w/o 10.2.93	J-626 w/o 13.6.86
J-200 w/o 28.2.91	J-629 w/o 15.4.86
J-206 w/o 15.6.01	J-634 w/o 28.5.84
J-216 w/o 10.3.80	J-639 w/o 11.2.88
J-217 w/o 17.7.81	J-645 w/o 10.8.93
J-224 w/o 26.4.83	J-710 w/o 21.11.90
J-225 w/o 21.3.83	J-865 w/o 3.6.85
J-227 w/o 26.4.83	J-880 w/o 21.5.91
J-233 w/o 20.10.81	
J-237 w/o 3.6.81	
J-238 w/o 18.12.92	**F-16B**
J-244 w/o 17.11.86	J-260 w/o 21.12.93
J-252 w/o 4.10.83	J-271 w/o 11.12.84

Above: No 316 Squadron only used the F-16 for a few years, having converted from Canadair NF-5s during 1991. The unit performed the OCU role during its brief existence although the squadron managed to celebrate its 40th anniversary during 1993. As part of a defence review, 316 was officially disbanding on April 1, 1994. (KEY Archive)

Right: Four 315 Squadron F-16A Block 15s of the Royal Netherlands Air Force in flight during 1996 – all four aircraft have the tail extension fitted to house a brake parachute. (RNlAF/Sgt1 Henk van Dijk)

Left and lower left: Every year the Dutch select one F-16 squadron to perform on the airshow circuit both at home and aboard. Each unit usually paints the designated display jet in a special colour scheme. Two very different 'paint jobs' are illustrated here – 322 Squadron at Leeuwarden painted J-364 in this scheme during 1997. For the 2001 display season, 312 Squadron at Volkel carried a rather striking and different scheme. (Both KEY – Duncan Cubitt)

Royal Netherlands AF
313 Squadron

Below: No 313 Squadron converted to the F-16 during 1989 after flying Canadair NF-5 Freedom Fighters while based at Twenthe in Holland. The squadron originally had a golden eagle for its unit badge; however to become a member of the NATO Tiger association it adopted a tiger's head instead. (RNIAF/Sgt1 Henk van Dijk)

Above: A Portuguese AF Vought A-7P Corsair II of 304 Esquadra escorting two F-16s of 322 Squadron along the Portuguese coastline during a squadron exchange before Portugal purchased F-16s. (Jelle Sjoerdsma)

Right: F-16B J-262 photographed flying alongside an aircraft type it was originally tasked with shooting down – in this case a Russian Knights Sukhoi Su-27UB *Flanker*. (KEY Archive)

Bottom: Another Lockheed Martin product, the F-117 Knighthawk follows an F-16A of 314 Squadron along the Dutch coast. Another victim of defence review cutbacks, 314 Squadron disbanded during July 1995. J-206 was later converted to an F-16AM – it was lost in a crash on June 15, 2001; the pilot ejecting safely. (KEY Archive)

Royal Netherlands AF
322 Squadron

Left: Two 313 Squadron F-16s fly a tight formation with a pair of Hungarian AF Mikoyan MiG-29s during an exchange visit to Kecskemét AB in Hungary during 1995. (RNlAF/Sgt1 Henk van Dijk)

Royal Netherlands AF
323 Squadron

Lower left: Six F-16AMs return to Holland after a detachment to the Canadian Air Base at Goose Bay, where the Dutch AF has been carrying out low-flying training since 1986.

Norway 331 Squadron

Below: No 332 Squadron became the first F-16 unit in Norway re-forming at Rygge alongside 331 Squadron, which moved to Bodø after becoming operational. F-16A 272 was the first production single-seat aircraft built for Norway, making its first flight on May 1, 1980. It is seen escorting a Panavia Tornado F.3 from 11 Squadron back to Rygge. This aircraft was still in service during 2001, and has been updated to MLU standard. (Ian Black)

NORWAY		
Royal Norwegian Air Force		
(Kongelige Norske Luftforsvaret)		
331 Skvadron	Bodø	F-16AM/BM
332 Skvadron	Rygge	F-16AM/BM
338 Skvadron	Ørland	F-16AM/BM
F-16A		
Block 01	272 to 274	78-0272 to 78-0274
Block 05	275 to 284	78-0275 to 78-0284
Block 10	285 to 299	78-0285 to 78-0299
Block 15	300	78-0300
	658 to 688	80-3658 to 80-3688
F-16B		
Block 01	301 to 302	78-0301 to 78-0302
Block 05	303 to 304	78-0303 to 78-0304
Block 10	305 to 307	78-0305 to 78-0307
Block 15	689 to 693	80-3689 to 80-3693
	711 to 712	87-0711 to 87-0712

Norway 332 Squadron

Norway 334 Squadron

Norway 338 Squadron

Below: Following the terrorist attacks in New York and Washington on September 11, 2001, Pakistan's President Musharraf supported the US-led war on terrorism, which resulted in substantial aid packages being made available to the new ally. At the same time, Pakistan also requested final release of the 28 F-16s embargoed since 1990. However the US Government has refused to release these and they remain in store at AMARC Davis-Monthan AFB. (KEY – Alan Warnes)

Right: During 2001 the Norwegian Government announced that 334 Squadron was to disband, its crews having already merged with 331 Squadron to ease an overall shortage of aircrew. At a later date the airfield at Rygge will be downgraded to 'reserve' status, for emergency use only. All the remaining F-16s will be split between the three surviving squadrons, with nine aircraft to be held in storage as reserves. (Ian Black)

Right: Norway postponed plans to purchase a new fighter aircraft during funding cutbacks announced in 2000. If the purchase had gone ahead, the Air Force would have ordered either 20 to 30 F-16 Block 50s, or a similar amount of Eurofighter EF2000 Typhoons. The government shelved its plans until after 2010, leaving the remaining upgraded F-16s to carry on until then. However, the government announced plans to assign several units to future international peace-keeping duties during 2001, these included F-16s from 338 Squadron illustrated here. (KEY Archive – 338 Skvadron)

NORWAY (continued)	
Losses	
F-16A	676 w/o 10.1.89
274 w/o 24.4.97	679 w/o 14.3.88
278 w/o 23.3.92	684 w/o 10.7.86
280 w/o 2.6.81	685 w/o 6.6.89
283 w/o 31.1.83	
287 w/o 5.4.89	**F-16B**
290 w/o 15.9.87	301 w/o 13.11.84
294 w/o 5.4.89	303 w/o 12.6.85
296 w/o 22.5.90	307 w/o 4.5.95
300 w/o 5.7.88	712 w/o 17.3.01

PAKISTAN	
Pakistani Air Force (Fiza Ya)	
9 Squadron	Sarghoda F-16A/B Block 15
11 Squadron	Sarghoda F-16A/B Block 15
F-16A Block 15	
82701 to 82702	81-0899 to 81-0900
83703	81-0901
84704 to 84719	81-0902 to 81-0917
85720 to 85728	81-0918 to 81-0926
91729	90-0942
92730 to 92734	90-0943 to 90-0947
92735 to 92738	92-0404 to 92-0407
93739 to 93741	92-0408 to 92-0410
93742 to 93782	92-0411 to 90-0451 (not built)
F-16B Block 15	
82601 to 82604	81-0931 to 81-0934
83605	81-0935
84606 to 84608	81-0936 to 81-0938
85609 to 85612	81-1504 to 81-1507
91613	90-0948
92614 to 92619	90-0949 to 90-0952
93620 to 93621	92-0452 to 92-0453
94622 to 94623	92-0456 to 92-0457
95624 to 95627	92-0458 to 92-0461
95628 to 95629	92-0462 to 92-0463 (not built)
Losses	
F-16A	**F-16B**
82701 w/o 22.10.94	84607 w/o 10.11.93
84712 w/o 4.9.89	85609 w/o 18.12.86
85720 w/o 2.5.87	??? w/o 6.9.95
85721 w/o 17.3.94	
85723 w/o 16.6.91	
85725 w/o 28.10.91	

PORTUGAL

Portuguese Air Force (Força Aérea Portuguesa)
Esquadra 201   *Falcões (Falcons)*
Monte Real   F-16A/B Block 15 OCU
A numberplate for the second squadron using the
ex-USAF F-16ADF is currently undecided

F-16A Block 15
15101 to 15117   93-0465 to 93-0481

F-16B Block 15
15118 to 15120   93-0482 to 93-0484

Surplus USAF aircraft

F-16A			
15121	82-0904	15134	82-1022
15122	82-0918	15135	83-1068
15123	82-0936	15136	83-1073
15124	82-0941	15137	83-1076
15125	82-0944	15138	83-1077
15126	82-0948	15139	83-1080
15127	82-0952	15140	83-1081
15128	82-0975	15141	83-1090
15129	82-0982	**F-16B**	
15130	82-0999	15142	81-0822
15131	82-1004	15143	83-1167
15132	82-1007	15144	83-1168
15133	82-1017	15145	83-1171

Above: Portugal has purchased 25 surplus USAF F-16s, previously stored at AMARC. The aircraft were shipped across the Atlantic Ocean, and were being prepared for Mid-Life Updates prior to entering service during 2002. (Lockheed Martin)

Left: Once the second unit of Portuguese F-16s has entered service, the current aircraft will undergo the MLU programme. The second batch will consist of four more F-16Bs, which will relieve the three F-16Bs currently in service. (Lockheed Martin)

Portuguese AF 201st Squadron

SINGAPORE

The Republic of Singapore Air Force
No 140 Squadron   Tengah   F-16A/B Block 15 OCU
   Osprey
No 143 Squadron   Tengah   F-16C/D Block 52
   Phoenix
Black Knights   Tengah   F-16A Block 15 OCU
   Aerobatic Team
(See under USAF for training units)

F-16A Block 15
880 to 883   87-0397 to 87-0400

F-16B Block 15
884 to 887   87-0401 to 87-0404

F-16C Block 52
608 to 615   94-0266 to 94-0273

            96-5025 to 96-5028
            97-0112 to 97-0121

F-16D Block 52
638	94-0274
623	94-0275
624	94-0276
625	94-0277
626	94-0278
627	94-0279
	94-0280 to 94-0283
	96-5029 to 96-5036
	97-0122 to 97-0123

Losses
F-16A   883 w/o 8.7.91

Singapore AF 140th Squadron

RoCAF 21st Tactical Fighter Squadron

Right: This Taiwanese F-16A is being prepared for an engine test inside a hush-house at Chiayi air base. The F-16s are operated by two wings and regularly fly alongside other Republic of China AF (RoCAF) fighters including the AIDC Ching-Kuo, Dassault Mirage 2000-5s and Northrop Grumman F-5 Tiger IIs. (KEY Archive)

Below: Seven of the original eight F-16A/B models survive in service with 140 (Osprey) Squadron of the Royal Singaporean AF (RSiAF). The eighth aircraft, an F-16A crashed during July 1991. One of the surviving F-16As has been converted into a technology demonstrator, sponsored by both the Ministry of Defence and the Air Force. It features upgrades to the cockpit and seen here on display at Asian Aerospace during February 2002. (Key – Alan Warnes)

TAIWAN

Republic of China AF (Chung-Kuo Kung Chuan)

4th Tactical Fighter Wing	Chiayi
4th Tactical Fighter Group	
14th Tactical Fighter Squadron	F-16A/B Block 20
21st Tactical Fighter Squadron	F-16A/B Block 20
22nd Tactical Fighter Squadron	F-16A/B Block 20
23rd Tactical Fighter Squadron	F-16A/B Block 20

5th Tactical Fighter Wing	Hualien
5th Tactical Fighter Group	
17th Tactical Fighter Squadron	F-16A/B Block 20
26th Tactical Fighter Squadron	F-16A/B Block 20

27th Tactical Fighter Squadron   F-16A/B Block 20
12th Tactical Reconnaissance Squadron
(Operates 12 standard F-16s carrying reconnaissance pods and several RF-16s modified by Singapore Technologies Aerospace)

F-16A Block 20	
6601 to 6720	93-0702 to 93-0821

F-16B Block 20	
6801 to 6830	93-0822 to 93-0851

Losses	
F-16A	**F-16B**
6638 w/o 1.6.99	6813 w/o 25.1.99
6680 w/o 18.8.99	6828 w/o 20.3.98

THAILAND		
Royal Thai Air Force (Kongtap Agard Thai)	**F-16A Block 15**	
	10305	86-0378
2nd Air Division	10306 to 10312	87-0702 to 87-0708
No 1 Wing Korat/Nakhon Ratchasima	40307 to 40318	90-7020 to 90-7031
103 Squadron F-16A/B Block 15	10313 to 10318	91-0062 to 91-0067
3rd Air Division	**F-16B Block 15**	
No 4 Wing Takhli	10301 to 10303	86-0379 to 86-0381
403 Squadron F-16A/B Block 15	10304	87-0709
Cobras	40301 to 40306	90-7032 to 90-7037

Thailand 4th Tactical Fighter Wing

Left: Thailand has purchased two batches of F-16 Block 15s – the last aircraft from the second batch was the 983rd and last Block 15 built. (Lockheed Martin)

Below: Thailand will receive 16 surplus US ANG F-16ADF aircraft during 2002, together with two Block 10 aircraft for spares recovery. (Lockheed Martin)

TURKEY			
Turkish Air Force (Türk Hava Kuvvetleri)		**6ncü Ana Hava Üs**	**Bandirma**
		161 Filo	F-16C/D Block 40
4ncü Ana Hava Üs	**Akinci**	162 Filo	F-16C/D Block 40
141 Filo	F-16C/D Block 40		
142 Filo	F-16C/D Block 30	**8ncü Ana Hava Üs**	**Diyarbakir**
Öncel Filo	F-16C/D Block 30	181 Filo	F-16C/D Block 40
		182 Filo	F-16C/D Block 40
5ncü Ana Hava Üs	**Merzifon**		
151 Filo	F-16C/D Block 50	**9ncü Ana Hava Üs**	**Balikesir**
152 Filo	F-16C/D Block 50	191 Filo	F-16C/D Block 40
		192 Filo	F-16C/D Block 40

Turkish 161st Fighter Squadron

TURKEY (continued)	
F-16C Block 30	**F-16D Block 30**
86-0066 to 86-0072	86-0191 to 86-0196
87-0009 to 87-0021	87-0002 to 87-0003
88-0019 to 88-0032	
	F-16D Block 40
F-16C Block 40	88-0013 to 88-0015
88-0033 to 88-0037	89-0042 to 89-0045
89-0022 to 89-0041	90-0022 to 90-0024
90-0001 to 90-0021	91-0022 to 91-0024
91-0001 to 91-0021	92-0022 to 92-0024
92-0001 to 92-0021	
93-0001 to 93-0014	**F-16D Block 50**
	93-0691 to 93-0696
F-16C Block 50	94-0105 to 94-0110
93-0657 to 93-0690	94-1557 to 94-1564
94-0071 to 94-0096	
Losses F-16C	
86-0067 w/o 5.7.91	91-0009 w/o 3.1.94
87-0012 w/o 25.6.92	91-0021 w/o 8.2.95
88-0022 w/o 7.5.95	91-0023 w/o 8.10.96
88-0023 w/o 11.10.95	??? w/o 25.7.97
89-0029 w/o 28.4.93	??? w/o 26.8.99
89-0033 w/o 29.9.95	??? w/o 4.4.00
90-0002 w/o 1.4.93	??? w/o 4.4.00
90-0003 w/o 22.11.94	??? w/o 24.5.00

Top right: 151 Squadron operates a mix of F-16C and D Block 50s in the SEAD role from Merzifon AB, close to the Black Sea. The squadron's badge depicts a vulture carrying an AGM-88 HARM. (KEY – Duncan Cubitt)

Right: Two F-16Cs line up on the end of the runway at Akinci near Ankara, during 1996. (KEY – Alan Warnes)

Lower right: A Turkish AF F-16C from 141 Squadron, flying over the Israeli desert during an official exchange visit, the aircraft is wearing the unit's wolf's head badge. The aircraft has been re-fitted with the AN/ALQ-178(V)3 Rapport III RWR/ECM – the antennas are visible under the nose and on the brake parachute housing. (Recep Demirkaya)

Turkish 9th Fighter Wing, 191st Squadron

USAF AIR COMBAT COMMAND

20th Fighter Wing 'SW'	Shaw AFB, South Carolina	F-16C/D
55th Fighter Squadron (blue)	Fightin'55th	Block 50
77th Fighter Squadron (red)	Gamblers	Block 50
78th Fighter Squadron (yellow/red)	Bushmasters	Block 50
79th Fighter Squadron (yellow/black)	Tigers	Block 50

27th Fighter Wing 'CC'	Cannon AFB, New Mexico	F-16C/D
428th Fighter Squadron (black) (Singaporean AF training unit)	Buccaneers	Block 52
522nd Fighter Squadron (red)	Fireballs	Block 30
523rd Fighter Squadron (blue)	Crusaders	Block 30
524th Fighter Squadron (yellow)	Hounds	Block 40

53rd Wing 'OT'	Eglin AFB, Florida	F-16C/D
49th Test & Evaluation Group		
85th Test & Evaluation Squadron		Block 30/40/42/50
422nd Test & Evaluation Squadron (Based at Nellis AFB, Nevada)	Green Bats	Block 42/52

57th Wing 'WA'	Nellis AFB, Nevada	F-16C/D
Fighter Weapons School		Block 42 & 52
414th CTS		Block 32/50/52
USAF Demonstration Team	The Thunderbirds	Block 32

366th Fighter Wing 'MO'	Mountain Home AFB, Idaho	F-16C/D
389th Fighter Squadron (red/yellow)	Thunderbolts	Block 52

388th Fighter Wing 'HL'	Hill AFB, Utah	F-16C/D
4th Fighter Squadron (yellow)		Block 40
34th Fighter Squadron (red)	Rude Rams	Block 40
421st Fighter Squadron (black)	Black Widows	Block 40

USAF MATERIAL COMMAND

46th Test Wing 'ET'	Eglin AFB, Florida	F-16A/B/C/D
39th Flight Test Squadron		Block /15/25/40/50

412th Test Wing 'ED'	Edwards AFB, California	
416th Flight Test Squadron		Blocks 15/25/30/40/42/50
Test Pilots School		
Combined Test Force		

USAF RESERVE COMMAND

301st Fighter Wing	NAS Fort Worth JRB, Texas	F-16C/D
457th Fighter Squadron	Spads	Block 30

419th Fighter Wing 'HI'	Hill AFB, Utah	F-16C/D
466th Fighter Squadron	Diamondbacks	Block 30

482nd Fighter Wing 'FM'	Homestead AFB, Florida	F-16C/D
93rd Fighter Squadron	Florida Makos	Block (32)?

944th Fighter Wing 'LR'	Luke AFB, Arizona	F-16C/D
302nd Fighter Squadron	Sun Devils	Block 32

USAF AIR EDUCATION AND TRAINING COMMAND

56th Fighter Wing 'LF'	Luke AFB, Phoenix, Arizona	F-16C/D
21st Fighter Squadron (white/red) (Taiwanese AF training unit)	Gamblers	F-16A/B Block 20
61st Fighter Squadron (yellow/black)	Top Dogs	Block 25
62nd Fighter Squadron (white/blue)	Spikes	Block 25
63rd Fighter Squadron (red/black)	Panthers	Block 42
308th Fighter Squadron (green/white)	Emerald Knights	Block 42
309th Fighter Squadron (blue/white)	Wild Ducks	Block 25
310th Fighter Squadron (green/yellow)	Top Hats	Block 42
425th Fighter Squadron (red/black) (Singaporean AF training unit)	Black Widows	Block 52

82nd Training Wing 'ST'	Sheppard AFB, Texas	
396th TTG		
Ground Instructional Training Airframes		
Block	10/15/25/32/40	

USAF OVERSEAS BASED UNITS

Pacific Air Force

8th Fighter Wing 'WP' Wolfpack	Kunsan AB, Korea	F-16C/D
35th Fighter Squadron (red)	Pantons	Block 40
80th Fighter Squadron (yellow)	Juvats	Block 30

35th Fighter Wing 'WW'	Misawa AB, Japan	F-16C/D
13th Fighter Squadron (red)	Panthers	Block 50
14th Fighter Squadron (yellow)	Samurai	Block 40

United States Air Forces Europe

31st Fighter Wing 'AV'	Aviano AB, Italy	F-16C/D
510th Fighter Squadron (purple)	Buzzards	Block 40
555th Fighter Squadron (green)	Triple Nickel	Block 40

52nd Fighter Wing 'SP'	Spangdahlem AB, Germany	F-16C/D
22nd Fighter Squadron (red)	Stingers	Block 50
23rd Fighter Squadron (blue)	Fighting Hawks	Block 50

MISCELLANEOUS UNITED STATES OPERATORS

National Air & Space Administration
Dryden Flight Research Centre (Edwards AFB), California. Operated two F-16XLs, though these are both currently in storage.

Lockheed Martin

Lockheed Fort Worth, Texas	F-16A/B/C/D
Company Trials Fleet	Various Blocks

Top left: The 1,000th F-16 built was still serving with the North Dakota ANG towards the end of 2001. A final retirement date for the remaining two F-16 ADF squadrons had not been announced, although one unit's worth of aircraft was slated for transfer to Thailand during 2002. (Lockheed Martin)

Centre left: F-16s still perform various flight test roles at Edwards AFB, and with no end to production, together with various upgrades planned, they look set to continue for many years. This 412th TW F-16B flies in formation with a Lockheed Martin F-22. (Lockheed Martin)

Bottom left: An F-16C Block 40 of the 388th FW stands alongside an aircraft that was developed from the loser of the original Lightweight Fighter (LWF) competition. The Northrop YF-17 design served as the basis for the Boeing (formerly McDonnell Douglas) F/A-18, the newest version of which, the F/A-18F Super Hornet, is also seen here.

Left: Five F-16s from the 79th FS at Shaw fly in formation while deploying to Buckley AFB, Colorado during August 2001. The squadron was participating in the first 'Tiger Meet of the Americas', which mirrors the NATO Tiger Meet. The 79th FS was a regular visitor to the European event when it operated General Dynamics F-111Es from RAF Upper Heyford in the United Kingdom. (USAF – S/Sgt Greg L Davis)

Below: The host unit for the 'Tiger Meet of the Americas' was the 120th FS, Colorado ANG, which painted one of its aircraft in this tiger scheme. (USAF – S/Sgt Greg L Davis)

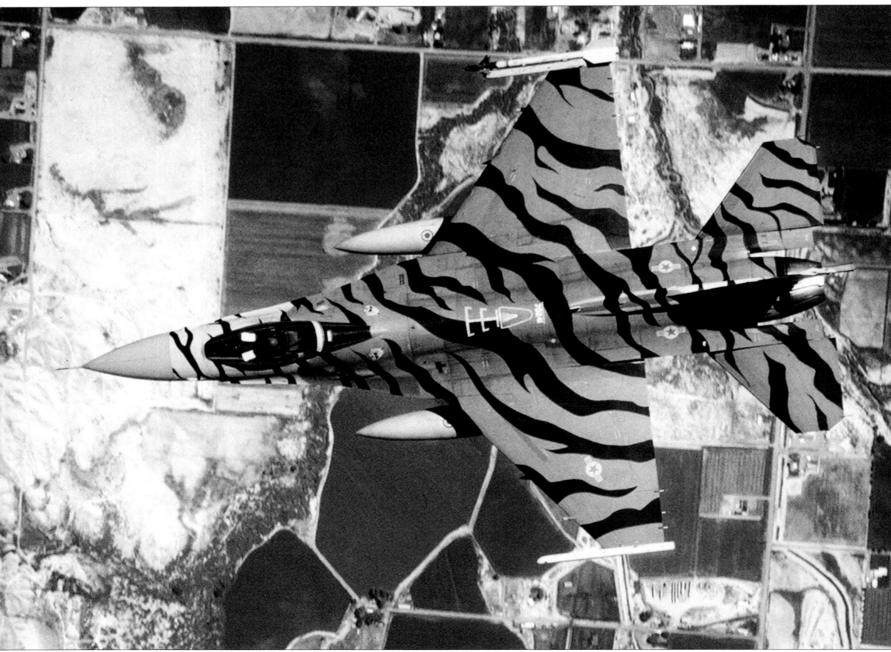

USAF AIR NATIONAL GUARD

113th Fighter Wing 'DC'	**Andrews AFB, Maryland**	**F-16C/D**
121st Fighter Squadron	*Capital Guardians*	Block 30
114th Fighter Wing	**Joe Foss Field, South Dakota**	**F-16C/D**
175th Fighter Squadron	*Lobos*	Block 30
115th Fighter Wing 'WI'	**Truax Field, Wisconsin**	**F-16C/D**
176th Fighter Squadron	*Badgers*	Block 30
119th Fighter Wing	**Hector IAP, North Dakota**	**F-16A/B**
178th Fighter Squadron	*Happy Hooligans*	ADF
120th Fighter Wing	**Great Falls IAP, Montana**	**F-16C/D**
186th Fighter Squadron		Block 30
122nd Fighter Wing 'FW'	**Fort Wayne IAP, Indiana**	**F-16C/D**
163rd Fighter Squadron	*Snakes*	Block 25
127th Wing 'MI'	**Selfridge ANGB, Michigan**	**F-16C/D**
(Due to gain a Reconnaissance tasking)		
107th Fighter Squadron	*Wolves*	Block 30
132nd Fighter Wing 'IA'	**Des Moines IAP, Iowa**	**F-16C/D**
124th Fighter Squadron	*Hawkeyes*	Block 42
138th Fighter Wing 'OK'	**Tulsa IAP, Oklahoma**	**F-16C/D**
125th Fighter Squadron		Block 42
140th Wing 'CO'	**Buckley ANGB, Colorado**	**F-16C/D**
120th Fighter Squadron	*Cougars*	Block 30
144th Fighter Wing	**Fresno-Yosemite ANGB, California**	**F-16C/D**
194th Fighter Squadron	*Griffins*	Block 25
(maintains a detachment at March ARB)		
147th Fighter Wing 'EF'	**Ellington Field, ANGB Texas**	**F-16C/D**
111th Fighter Squadron	*Ace in the Hole*	Block 25
148th Fighter Wing 'MN'	**Duluth IAP, Minnesota**	**F-16A/B**
179th Fighter Squadron	*Bulldogs*	ADF
(Plus detachment at Tyndall AFB)		
149th Fighter Wing 'SA'	**Kelly AFB, Texas**	**F-16C/D**
182nd Fighter Squadron	*Gunfighters*	Block 30

150th Fighter Wing 'NM'	**Kirtland AFB, New Mexico**	**F-16C/D**
188th Fighter Squadron	*Tacos*	Block 30 & 40
158th Fighter Wing 'VT'	**Burlington IAP, Vermont**	**F-16C/D**
134th Fighter Squadron	*Green Mountain Boys*	Block 25
162nd Fighter Wing (Reports to AETC)	**Tucson IAP, Arizona**	**F-16A/B/C/D**
148th Fighter Squadron	*Kickin' Ass*	Block 15
152nd Fighter Squadron	*Tigers*	Block 25/42
195th Fighter Squadron	*Warhawks*	Block 10
AFRC & ANG Test Centre		Block 25
169th Fighter Wing 'SC'	**McEntire ANGB, South Carolina**	**F-16C/D**
157th Fighter Squadron	*Swamp Foxes*	Block 52
174th Fighter Wing 'NY'	**Hancock Field, Syracuse, New York**	**F-16C/D**
138th Fighter Squadron		Block 25

The 174th FW works closely with the USAF's Rome Laboratory to test improvements and modifications developed for the F-16.

177th Fighter Wing 'AC'	**Atlantic City, New Jersey**	**F-16C/D**
119th Fighter Squadron	*Jersey Devils*	Block 25
178th Fighter Wing 'OH'	**Springfield-Beckley MAP, Ohio**	**F-16C/D**
162nd Fighter Squadron	*Sabers*	Block 30
180th Fighter Wing 'OH'	**Toledo Express AP, Ohio**	**F-16C/D**
112th Fighter Squadron	*Stingers*	Block 42
181st Fighter Wing 'TH'	**Hulman Field, Terre Haute AP, Indiana**	**F-16C/D**
113th Fighter Squadron	*Racers*	Block 30
183rd Fighter Wing 'SI'	**Capitol MAP, Illinois**	**F-16C/D**
170th Fighter Squadron	*Flyin' Ilini*	Block 30
185th Fighter Wing 'HA'	**Sioux Gateway AP, Sioux City, Iowa**	**F-16C/D**
174th Fighter Squadron	*Bats*	Block 30
187th Fighter Wing 'AL'	**Dannelly Field, Alabama**	**F-16C/D**
160th Fighter Squadron	*Snakes*	Block 30
188th Fighter Wing 'FS'	**Fort Smith MAP, Arkansas**	**F-16A/B**
184th Fighter Squadron	*Razorbacks*	ADF
192nd Fighter Wing 'VA'	**Bryd Field, Richmond IAP, Vermont**	**F-16C/D**
149th Fighter Squadron		Block 30

Air Combat Command

Air National Guard

PROTOTYPES AND DEVELOPMENT AIRCRAFT

Prototypes	
YF-16	72-1067 and 72-1068

Full-Scale Development Aircraft	
F-16A	75-0745 to 75-0750
F-16B	75-0751 to 75-0752

USA PRODUCTION

F-16A Block 01
78-001 to 78-0021

F-16A Block 5
78-0022 to 78-0027
78-0038 to 78-0076
79-0288 to 79-0331

F-16A Block 10
79-0332 to 79-0409
80-0474 to 80-0540

F-16A Block 15
80-0541 to 80-0622
81-0663 to 81-0811
82-0900 to 82-1025
83-1066 to 83-1117

F-16B Block 1
78-0077 to 78-0098

F-16B Block 5
78-0099 to 78-0115
79-0410 to 79-0419

F-16B Block 10
79-0420 to 79-0432
80-0623 to 80-0634

F-16B Block 15
80-0635 to 80-0638
81-0812 to 81-0822
82-1026 to 82-1042
82-1044 to 82-1049
83-1166 to 83-1173

F-16C Block 25
83-1118 to 83-1165
84-1212 to 84-1318
84-1374 to 84-1395
85-1399
85-1401
85-1403 to 85-1407
85-1409
85-1411
85-1413
85-1415 to 85-1421
85-1423
85-1425
85-1427
85-1429 to 85-1431
85-1433
85-1435
85-1437
85-1439
85-1441
85-1443
85-1445
85-1447
85-1452

F-16C Block 30
85-1398
85-1400
85-1402
85-1408
85-1410
85-1412
85-1414
85-1422
85-1424
85-1426

85-1428
85-1432
85-1434
85-1436
85-1438
85-1440
85-1442
85-1444
85-1446
85-1448 to 85-1451
85-1453 to 85-1505
85-1544 to 85-1570
86-0207 to 86-0209
86-0216
86-0219
86-0221 to 86-0235
86-0237
86-0242 to 86-0249
86-0254 to 86-0255
86-0258 to 86-0268
86-0270
86-0274 to 86-0278
86-0282
86-0284
86-0286 to 86-0290
86-0293 to 86-0295
86-0297 to 86-0298
86-0300 to 86-0371
87-0217 to 87-0266
87-0270 to 87-0292
87-0294
87-0296
87-0298
87-0300
87-0302
87-0304
87-0306
87-0308
87-0310
87-0312
87-0314
87-0316
87-0318
87-0320
87-0322
87-0324
87-0326
87-0328
87-0330
87-0332
87-0334 to 87-0349
88-0397 to 88-0411

F-16C Block 32
86-0210 to 86-0215
86-0217 to 86-0218
86-0220
86-0236
86-0238 to 86-0241
86-0250 to 86-0253
86-0256 to 86-0257
86-0269
86-0279 to 86-0281
86-0283
86-0285
86-0291 to 86-0292
86-0296
86-0299
87-0267
87-0269
87-0293
87-0295

87-0297
87-0299
87-0301
87-0303
87-0305
87-0307
87-0309
87-0311
87-0313
87-0315
87-0317
87-0319
87-0321
87-0323
87-0325
87-0327
87-0329
87-0331
87-0333

F-16C Block 40
87-0350 to 87-0355
87-0357
87-0359
88-0413
88-0415 to 88-0416
88-0418 to 88-0419
88-0421 to 88-0422
88-0424 to 88-0426
88-0428 to 88-0433
88-0435 to 88-0441
88-0443 to 88-0444
88-0446 to 88-0447
88-0449 to 88-0450
88-0452 to 88-0454
88-0456 to 88-0457
88-0459 to 88-0460
88-0462 to 88-0463
88-0465 to 88-0468
88-0470 to 88-0471
88-0473 to 88-0474
88-0476 to 88-0477
88-0479 to 88-0480
88-0482 to 88-0483
88-0485 to 88-0486
88-0488 to 88-0489
88-0491 to 88-0492
88-0494 to 88-0495
88-0497 to 88-0498
88-0500 to 88-0501
88-0503 to 88-0504
88-0506 to 88-0507
88-0509 to 88-0510
88-0512 to 88-0513
88-0515 to 88-0516
88-0518 to 88-0519
88-0521 to 88-0523
88-0525 to 88-0526
88-0528 to 88-0529
88-0531 to 88-0533
88-0535 to 88-0538
88-0540 to 88-0541
88-0543 to 88-0544
88-0546 to 88-0547
88-0549 to 88-0550
89-2000 to 89-2001
89-2003
89-2005 to 89-2006
89-2008 to 89-2009
89-2011
89-2013 to 89-2016
89-2018

89-2020 to 89-2021
89-2023 to 89-2024
89-2026 to 89-2027
89-2029 to 89-2030
89-2032 to 89-2033
89-2035 to 89-2036
89-2038 to 89-2039
89-2041 to 89-2044
89-2046 to 89-2047
89-2049 to 89-2050
89-2052
89-2054 to 89-2055
89-2057 to 89-2058
89-2060 to 89-2069
89-2071 to 89-2072
89-2074 to 89-2075
89-2077 to 89-2078
89-2080 to 89-2081
89-2083 to 89-2084
89-2086 to 89-2087
89-2090
89-2092 to 89-2093
89-2095 to 89-2096
89-2099
89-2101 to 89-2102
89-2104 to 89-2105
89-2108
89-2110 to 89-2111
89-2113
89-2115 to 89-2116
89-2118 to 89-2119
89-2121 to 89-2122
89-2124 to 89-2125
89-2127
89-2130 to 89-2131
89-2133 to 89-2134
89-2136 to 89-2137
89-2139 to 89-2140
89-2143 to 89-2144
89-2146 to 89-2147
89-2149 to 89-2150
89-2152 to 89-2153
90-0703
90-0709 to 90-0711
90-0714
90-0717 to 90-0718
90-0723 to 90-0725
90-0733 to 90-0736
90-0742 to 90-0745
90-0753
90-0756
90-0763
90-0771 to 90-0776

F-16C Block 42
87-0356
87-0358
88-0412
88-0414
88-0417
88-0420
88-0423
88-0427
88-0434
88-0442
88-0445
88-0448
88-0451
88-0455
88-0458
88-0461
88-0464

88-0469
88-0472
88-0475
88-0478
88-0481
88-0484
88-0487
88-0490
88-0493
88-0496
88-0499
88-0502
88-0505
88-0508
88-0511
88-0514
88-0517
88-0520
88-0524
88-0527
88-0530
88-0534
88-0539
88-0542
88-0545
88-0548
89-2002
89-2004
89-2007
89-2010
89-2012
89-2017
89-2019
89-2022
89-2025
89-2028
89-2031
89-2034
89-2037
89-2040
89-2045
89-2048
89-2051
89-2053
89-2056
89-2059
89-2070
89-2073
89-2076
89-2079
89-2082
89-2085
89-2088 to 89-2089
89-2091
89-2094
89-2097 to 89-2098
89-2100
89-2103
89-2106 to 89-2107
89-2109
89-2112
89-2114
89-2117
89-2120
89-2123
89-2126
89-2128 to 89-2129
89-2132
89-2135
89-2138
89-2141 to 89-2142
89-2145
89-2148

89-2151
89-2154
90-0700 to 90-0702
90-0704 to 90-0708
90-0712 to 90-0713
90-0715 to 90-0716
90-0719 to 90-0722
90-0726 to 90-0732
90-0737 to 90-0741
90-0746 to 90-0752
90-0754 to 90-0755
90-0757 to 90-0762
90-0764 to 90-0770

F-16C Block 50
90-0801 to 90-0808
90-0810 to 90-0833
91-0336 to 91-0361
91-0363 to 91-0369
91-0371 to 91-0373
91-0375 to 91-0385
91-0387 to 91-0391
91-0394 to 91-0400
91-0402 to 91-0403
91-0405 to 91-0412
91-0414 to 91-0423
92-3883 to 92-3884
92-3886 to 92-3887
92-3891 to 92-3895
92-3897
92-3900 to 92-3901
92-3904
92-3906 to 92-3907
92-3910
92-3912 to 92-3913
92-3915
92-3918 to 92-3921
92-3923
93-0532
93-0534
93-0536
93-0538
93-0540
93-0542
93-0544
93-0546
93-0548
93-0550
93-0552
93-0554
94-0038 to 94-0049
96-0080 to 96-0085
97-0106 to 97-0111
98-0003 to 98-0005
99-0082

F-16C Block 52
90-0809
91-0362
91-0370
91-0374
91-0386
91-0392 to 91-0393
91-0401
91-0404
91-0413
92-3880 to 92-03882
92-03885
92-3888 to 92-03890
92-3896

USA PRODUCTION (continued)

			F-16D Block 40	F-16D Block 42	F-16D Block 50
92-3998 to 92-3999	93-0551	86-0042 to 86-0047	87-0391 to 87-0393	87-0394 to 87-0396	90-0834 to 90-0838
92-3902 to 92-3903	93-0553		88-0166	88-0153 to 88-0165	90-0840 to 90-0849
92-3905		**NF-16D VISTA**	88-0168	88-0167	91-0462 to 91-0465
92-3908 to 92-3909	**F-16D Block 25**	86-0048	88-0170 to 88-0171	88-0169	91-0468 to 91-0469
92-3911	83-1174 to 83-1185		88-0174	88-0172 to 88-0173	91-0471 to 91-0472
92-3914	84-1319 to 84-1331	**F-16D Block 30**	89-2166	88-0175	91-0474
92-3916 to 92-3917	84-1396 to 84-1397	86-0049 to 86-0053	89-2168 to 89-2169	89-2155 to 89-2165	91-0476 to 91-0477
92-3922	85-1506 to 85-1508	87-0363 to 87-0368	89-2171 to 89-2174	89-2167	91-0480 to 91-0481
93-0531	85-1510	87-0370 to 87-0380	89-2176	89-2170	
93-0533	85-1512	87-0382 to 87-0390	89-2178	89-2175	**F-16D Block 52**
93-0535	85-1514 to 85-1516	88-0150 to 88-0152	90-0777	89-2177	90-0839
93-0537			90-0779 to 90-0780	89-2179	91-0466 to 91-0467
93-0539		**F-16D Block 32**	90-0782	90-0778	91-0470
93-0541	**F-16D Block 30**	86-0039 to 86-0041	90-0784	90-0781	91-0473
93-0543	85-1509	87-0369	90-0791 to 90-0792	90-0783	91-0475
93-0545	85-1511	87-0381	90-0794 to 90-0800	90-0785 to 90-0790	91-0478 to 91-0479
93-0547	85-1513			90-0793	92-3924 to 92-3927
93-0549	85-1517				
	85-1571 to 85-1573				

Right: Air Education and Training Command is responsible for all initial F-16 aircrew training and all new personnel report to the 56th FW at Luke AFB. The 308th FS is one of nine units attached to this wing. (USAF – S/A Jeffrey Allen)

Below: Another favourite decoration used by aviation units throughout the world, is the shark's mouth. Several F-16 units have carried these over the years – one is seen here applied to an F-16C of the 27th FW, during Exercise Roving Sands 97. (USAF – S/A Jeffrey Allen)

Left: The 148th FW Minnesota ANG were one of two Air National Guard units that were still operating the F-16 ADF during 2002. All the aircraft have the squadron nick-name painted on the fuselage. (USAF – M/Sgt Daniel J Schiles)

Centre left: F-16CJs of the 20th FW sit on the ramp at Shaw AFB, after a heavy snowfall during January 2002. (USAF – S/Sgt Greg L Davis)

Bottom: The USAF Air Demonstration Squadron, the Thunderbirds, in formation over the Grand Canyon during a practice display. The United States Air Force 306th Aerial Demonstration Squadron was initially formed at Luke AFB on May 25, 1953, with the Republic F-84 Thunderjet. Since then, the Thunderbirds team has flown most of the front-line types in the air force inventory. In 1956, while converting to the F-100, it moved to its current home at Nellis AFB, Nevada. After flying aircraft such as the F-4, F-105 and T-38, it converted to the F-16A/B in 1982 and today flies the F-16C/D. (USAF – S/Sgt Kevin Gruenwald)

USAF ANG 125th Fighter Squadron

USAF ANG 148th Fighter Squadron

152nd Fighter Squadron

USAF ANG188th Fighter Wing

457th Fighter Squadron

USA LOSSES

F-16A

78-0002 w/o 29.11.88
78-0004 w/o 11.2.85
78-0006 w/o 1.10.79
78-0009 w/o 24.1.91
78-0013 w/o 6.4.81
78-0016 w/o 12.4.82
78-0023 w/o 25.3.80
78-0041 w/o 22.3.80
78-0045 w/o 22.3.80
78-0046 w/o 5.8.81
78-0048 w/o 15.1.82
78-0055 w/o 12.2.86
78-0067 w/o 11.5.82
78-0071 w/o 25.6.80
78-0072 w/o 19.6.84
78-0075 w/o 10.10 86
79-0298 w/o 8.11.82
79-0301 w/o 20.5.82
79-0313 w/o 29.6.81
79-0315 w/o 10.4.84
79-0316 w/o 10.4.81
79-0318 w/o 27.1.82
79-0323 w/o 7.2.85
79-0338 w/o 9.9.88
79-0343 w/o 27.12.82
79-0350 w/o 18.11.83
79-0367 w/o 11.3.86
79-0372 w/o 1.11.85
79-0374 w/o 20.5.82
79-0378 w/o 16.6.82
79-0379 w/o 21.4.93
79-0385 w/o 22.6.87
79-0386 w/o 19.1.83
79-0390 w/o 4.5.82
79-0391 w/o 11.4.91
79-0392 w/o 9.6.82
79-0397 w/o 22.3.88
79-0398 w/o 28.6.89
79-0400 w/o 13.1.91
80-0477 w/o 25.9.84
80-0478 w/o 10.2.83
80-0484 w/o 27.11.91
80-0486 w/o 28.2.94
80-0490 w/o 6.7.82
80-0536 w/o 24.1.91
80-0564 w/o 1.12.82
80-0566 w/o 18.9.92
80-0574 w/o 20.5.88
80-0586 w/o 22.10.85
80-0595 w/o 25.1.84
80-0597 w/o 24.7.87
80-0599 w/o 11.9.86
80-0600 w/o 12.1.83
80-0605 w/o 2.7.96
80-0606 w/o 30.7.85
80-0610 w/o 5.5.92
80-0617 w/o 20.1.83
81-0664 w/o 10.5.83
81-0671 w/o 14.9.89
81-0684 w/o 7.1.97
81-0692 w/o 16.11.82
81-0697 w/o 31.8.92
81-0704 w/o 3.3.92
81-0706 w/o 3.3.92
81-0717 w/o 26.1.91
81-0724 w/o 15.12.82
81-0730 w/o 27.1.84
81-0745 w/o 1.5.84
81-0747 w/o 26.4.86
81-0750 w/o 8.8.85
81-0758 w/o 3.4.91
81-0766 w/o 11.3.88

81-0770 w/o 29.11.93
81-0779 w/o 11.9.93
81-0798 w/o 25.5.90
81-0808 w/o 8.2.85
82-0909 w/o 10.2.88
82-0912 w/o 24.7.87
82-0920 w/o 18.4.91
82-0925 w/o 10.11.83
82-0927 w/o 17.12.93
82-0934 w/o 12.6.94
82-0937 w/o 16.3.90
82-0939 w/o 21.10.85
82-0940 w/o 15.11.85
82-0943 w/o 31.7.92
82-0954 w/o 16.8.89
82-0959 w/o 21.11.84
82-0965 w/o 23.5.89
82-0971 w/o 25.6.84
82-0985 w/o 30.10.90
82-0990 w/o 27.8.93
82-0994 w/o 13.9.88
82-0998 w/o 9.10.86
82-1003 w/o 15.3.91
82-1015 w/o 13.1.88
82-1018 w/o 21.7.95
82-1020 w/o 22.11.96
83-1067 w/o 17.12.87
83-1071 w/o 21.5.92
83-1078 w/o 17.12.92
83-1082 w/o 17.11.89
83-1086 w/o 27.2.86
83-1089 w/o 14.1.91
83-1102 w/o 19.2.93
83-1115 w/o 22.3.87
83-1116 w/o 4.1.89
83-1117 w/o 27.4.85

F-16B

78-0078 w/o 9.8.79
78-0092 w/o 23.7.80
78-0093 w/o 15.5.95
78-0100 w/o 17.7.01
78-0105 w/o 27.3.81
78-0110 w/o 29.10.80
78-0112 w/o 23.3.82
78-0113 w/o 25.7.83
79-0416 w/o 16.5.85
79-0419 w/o 14.11.91
80-0627 w/o 11.7.83
81-0814 w/o 9.6.91
82-1029 w/o 15.11.85
82-1037 w/o 22.8.97
82-1038 w/o 23.5.86
82-1040 w/o 19.12.91
82-1042 w/o 23.6.93
82-1045 w/o 2.5.84
83-1173 w/o 1.7.94

F-16C

83-1133 w/o 10.1.02
83-1134 w/o 29.1.97
83-1138 w/o 31.8.00
83-1139 w/o 1.9.92
83-1149 w/o 25.7.87
83-1151 w/o 3.9.90
84-1217 w/o 25.10.01
84-1218 w/o 17.2.91
84-1221 w/o 2.8.88
84-1224 w/o 11.2.86
84-1228 w/o 5.1.89
84-1232 w/o 25.7.88
84-1233 w/o 12.11.86
84-1249 w/o 9.10.86

84-1250 w/o 21.12.95
84-1255 w/o 20.6.97
84-1259 w/o 9.10.86
84-1263 w/o 18.12.89
84-1267 w/o 13.1.92
84-1268 w/o 1.7.99
84-1270 w/o 10.10.87
84-1293 w/o 18.12.89
84-1304 w/o 3.2.99
84-1311 w/o 16.6.00
84-1314 w/o 15.12.98
84-1379 w/o 15.2.91
84-1389 w/o 13.3.88
84-1390 w/o 27.2.91
84-1395 w/o 29.6.88
85-1399 w/o 17.9.87
85-1401 w/o 29.6.88
85-1414 w/o 1.9.88
85-1423 w/o 28.1.91
85-1424 w/o 23.6.87
85-1451 w/o 8.9.92
85-1456 w/o 28.8.00
85-1462 w/o 18.4.88
85-1463 w/o 19.10.87
85-1485 w/o 22.10.92
85-1489 w/o 17.11.98
85-1492 w/o 28.4.93
85-1496 w/o 22.1.92
85-1545 w/o 7.6.96
85-1550 w/o 13.5.98
86-0213 w/o 20.2.88
86-0226 w/o 26.7.01
86-0247 w/o 29.6.88
86-0250 w/o 10.8.93
86-0253 w/o 27.9.93
86-0257 w/o 18.3.97
86-0274 w/o 14.2.89
86-0284 w/o 12.7.99
86-0297 w/o 29.1.89
86-0300 w/o 26.12.89
86-0311 w/o 14.3.89
86-0312 w/o 14.3.89
86-0313 w/o 13.12.00
86-0316 w/o 5.12.88
86-0325 w/o 9.11.93
86-0329 w/o 20.2.91
86-0343 w/o 11.8.93
86-0344 w/o 18.10.88
86-0354 w/o 23.10.90
86-0361 w/o 19.3.96
87-0224 w/o 21.1.91
87-0228 w/o 19.1.91
87-0240 w/o 17.11.99
87-0257 w/o 19.1.91
87-0269 w/o 18.5.93
87-0270 w/o 26.1.94
87-0273 w/o 25.6.95
87-0274 w/o 6.5.94
87-0302 w/o 7.5.91
87-0309 w/o 14.2.94
87-0330 w/o 21.3.01
87-0335 w/o 27.7.93
87-0357 w/o 21.6.00
88-0403 w/o 11.8.99
88-0408 w/o 3.4.90
88-0411 w/o 3.3.94
88-0414 w/o 22.10.98
88-0426 w/o 28.11.95
88-0448 w/o 8.11.93
88-0449 w/o 17.1.98
88-0450 w/o 9.11.98
88-0453 w/o 13.3.91
88-0455 w/o 21.8.95
88-0461 w/o 1.12.90

88-0470 w/o 14.1.92
88-0473 w/o 23.4.98
88-0478 w/o 10.2.95
88-0483 w/o 8.1.91
88-0488 w/o 21.9.94
88-0490 w/o 26.3.99
88-0519 w/o 24.8.98
88-0523 w/o 23.2.93
88-0542 w/o 8.8.00
88-0550 w/o 2.5.99
89-2000 w/o 5.2.95
89-2027 w/o 19.9.90
89-2032 w/o 2.6.95
89-2036 w/o 21.1.95
89-2050 w/o 18.7.01
89-2059 w/o 3.10.91
89-2061 w/o 4.4.91
89-2063 w/o 12.6.01
89-2069 w/o 18.5.93
89-2079 w/o 20.1.96
89-2088 w/o 12.10.00
89-2089 w/o 16.12.91
89-2093 w/o 31.7.96
89-2094 w/o 16.2.00
89-2095 w/o 21.4.97
89-2101 w/o 23.8.96
89-2104 w/o 16.11.00
89-2110 w/o 24.4.92
89-2131 w/o 8.1.98
89-2153 w/o 12.5.97
90-0749 w/o 31.5.92
90-0761 w/o 27.10.92
90-0764 w/o 7.2.94
90-0801 w/o 13.11.00
90-0804 w/o 24.7.98
90-0811 w/o 13.11.00
90-0814 w/o 25.10.94
90-0815 w/o 6.7.01
90-0823 w/o 8.2.94
90-0832 w/o 24.5.93
91-0350 w/o 8.10.93
91-0354 w/o 11.7.96
91-0397 w/o 22.7.98
92-3900 w/o 21.1.99
93-0534 w/o 19.3.00
93-0538 w/o 19.11.98

F-16D

83-1179 w/o 20.9.99
83-1320 w/o 16.9.97
83-1321 w/o 7.8.90
85-1510 w/o 20.9.90
85-1517 w/o 27.8.87
86-0040 w/o 12.9.98
86-0045 w/o 17.7.91
87-0363 w/o 15.3.89
87-0369 w/o 15.10.89
87-0372 w/o 27.11.96
87-0385 w/o 4.2.97
87-0389 w/o 4.12.98
87-0396 w/o 18.6.99
88-0154 w/o 7.1.99
88-0160 w/o 2.6.92
88-0167 w/o 23.7.01
88-0168 w/o 30.7.91
88-0171 w/o 23.3.94
89-2175 w/o 26.4.99
90-0784 w/o 18.2.93
90-0792 w/o 25.3.93
90-0794 w/o 16.2.00
90-0798 w/o 19.6.98
90-0837 w/o 3.4.01
90-0849 w/o 13.1.95

Above: In December 1996, the USAF 388th Fighter Wing passed five million flying hours of USAF flight-testing with the F-16. Captain Kurt Gallegos flew the milestone sortie during an aerial demonstration at Hill AFB, Utah. To commemorate the occasion, these special markings were applied. (Lockheed Martin)

USAF ANG 119th Fighter Squadron

Left: Based at Atlantic City International Airport, the 177th FW New Jersey ANG operates F-16 Block 25s, and like several ANG units, it now wears codes that refer to its home base. (USAF – M/Sgt Don Taggart)

Right: Weapons loaders from the 192nd FW Virginia ANG perform last-chance checks on an F-16C prior to it departing on a mission as part of Operation Noble Eagle. (USAF – S/A Michele G Misiano)

USAF ANG 162nd Fighter Squadron

Below: Both of the 52nd FW squadrons are represented here, together with the Wing Commander's aircraft. All three special scheme aircraft are seen in formation near Spangdahlem. (USAF – M/Sgt Blake R Borsic)

USA FOREIGN MILITARY SALES EXPORT PROGRAMME NAMES			
Bahrain	Peace Crown	Portugal	Peace Atlantis
Egypt	Peace Vector	Korea	Peace Bridge
Greece	Peace Xenia	Singapore	Peace Carvin
Indonesia	Peace Bima-Sena	Thailand	Peace Naresuan
Iran	Peace Zebra	Turkey	Peace Oynx
Israel	Peace Marble	Taiwan	Peace Fenghuang
Italy	Peace Caesar		
Jordan	Peace Falcon		
Pakistan	Peace Gate	Venezuela	Peace Delta

UNITED STATES NAVY	
F-16N Block 30	
163268 to 163277	85-1369 to 85-1378
163566 to 163577	86-1684 to 86-1695
TF-16N Block 30	
163278 to 163281	85-1379 to 85-1382
Losses	
163568 w/o 17.12.92	
163573 w/o 5.12.94	

USAF ANG 178th Fighter Squadron

USAF ANG 138th Fighter Squadron

USAF ANG 180th Fighter Squadron

Left: Three F-16s from the 414th CTS fly over the Nevada desert during a Red Flag exercise, the unit is part of the 57th Wing based at Nellis AFB. (Rick Llinares)

Left: Four 510th FS F-16Cs return to Zaragoza airbase after a successful mission during a weapon training deployment to Spain in February 2002. (USAF – T/Sgt Dave Ahlschwede)

Right: The Venezuelan AF has operated 24 F-16s since 1983, and maintains an excellent safety record. – they have only lost three aircraft. The F-16s have also undergone numerous upgrades and are able to carry the Rafael Litening pod. (KEY Archive)

Above: An F-16C from the 93rd FS flies along the southern Florida coastline near Homestead Air Reserve Base. (USAF – M/Sgt Joe Cupido)

Left: The 20th FW at Shaw AFB celebrated the 10th anniversary of the end of Operation Desert Storm during February 2001. The base held an airshow and painted an aircraft in the markings of the 363rd TFW, thus representing the wing under its previous designation. (USAF – S/Sgt Greg L Davis)

Venezuela Grupo 16

VENEZUELA

Fuerza Aérea Venezolana
Grupo Aero de Caza No 16 'Dragones', BA El Libertador, Palo Negro

| Escuadrón de Caza 161 *Caribes* | F-16A/B Block 15 |
| Escuadrón de Caza 162 *Gavilanes* | F-16A/B Block 15 |

F-16A Block 15			
1041	82-1050	0094	84-1349
0051	82-1051	6023	84-1350
6611	82-1052	4226	84-1351
9068	83-1186	5422	84-1352
0678	83-1187	6426	84-1353
3260	83-1188	4827	84-1354
7268	84-1346	9864	84-1355
8900	84-1347	3648	84-1356
8924	84-1348	0220	84-1357

F-16B Block 15			
1715	82-1053	2337	83-1189
2179	82-1054	7635	83-1190
9581	82-1055	9583	83-1191

Losses

F-16A	F-16B
6611 w/o 27.9.01	2179 w/o 16.11.95
	9581 w/o 20.4.94

⑨ F-16 IN COMBAT

Fighting Falcons have earned their spurs in combat – the last 20 years have seen them in action during the course of several wars and a number of more minor skirmishes. Israel has used the F-16 in various campaigns since its early days of service. On June 6, 1981, before deliveries of the first batch had been completed, eight aircraft took part in Operation Babylon, which involved flying into Iraqi airspace at low level to bomb the nuclear reactor under construction at Osirak, to the southeast of Baghdad, using precision guided munitions.

Israeli F-16s have taken part in all the operations over Lebanon against the Palestinian Liberation Organisation (PLO) and other organisations, including HAMAS. Israeli F-16s have also made the largest number of air-to-air kills; these were all against various Syrian Air Force types, over the Beka'a Valley during 1982.

The Pakistani Air Force became the second country to use its F-16s in anger, shooting down several aircraft that had violated its airspace during the Soviet occupation of Afghanistan. The following shoot-downs took place between May 1986 and November 1988. Three aircraft were shot down by 9 Squadron based at Sargodha, which was also the first unit to re-form on the F-16 within the Pakistani Air Force. These included a Sukhoi Su-22 confirmed as shot down on May 17, 1986; another was quoted as being a probable kill. No.9 Squadron was also responsible for shooting down an Antonov An-26 on March 30, 1987. No.14 Squadron, based at Kamra, claimed the remaining kills, which included one Su-22 and a Mikoyan MiG-23 on April 22, 1987.

The next kill to be claimed by the squadron was the only Soviet Air Force aircraft to fall to the PAF. On August 4, 1988, a 14 Squadron F-16A shot down a Sukhoi Su-25 being flown by Colonel Alexander Rutskoi, while in Pakistan airspace. Colonel Rutskoi had already escaped one previous encounter with an F-16, which fired two AIM-9s at his aircraft, during the shootdown on August 4. Colonel Rutsoki managed to eject from the stricken aircraft and was captured – he initially believed he had suffered a technical problem, and refused to accept that he had actually been shot down from behind with an AIM-9 Sidewinder. A wing section from his aircraft was later put on display at 14 Squadron's base at Kamra. Colonel Rutskoi was released after two weeks and went on to serve briefly as the President of the Russian Federation. The three remaining kills are credited to the same pilot,

who shot down two MiG-23s on September 12, 1988, together with an Su-22 on November 3 the same year.

The USAF deployed 249 Fighting Falcons during Operation Desert Storm. Active duty air force units flew F-16Cs, and ANG units from New York and South Carolina flew F-16As – though the latter only took part in air-to-ground operations.

The Venezuelan AF has three kills to its credit, all resulting from a brief political coup on November 27, 1992. This was the second attempted coup that year; the first, in February, had been led by Lieutenant Colonel Hugo Chavez, and was quickly quashed. (Chavez eventually

Left: Photographed on March 31, 1999, after breaking away from a USAF 100th Air Expeditionary Wing KC-135R during Operation Allied Force, this Dutch F-16 is carrying four AIM-9L Sidewinders, two CBU-87 cluster bombs, an AN/ALQ-131 ECM pod and long-range drop tanks. (USAF – T/Sgt Brad Fallin)

Below: A mix of Belgian F-16s from Florennes and Kleine Brogel are pictured at Amendola AB, Italy, on the flight line between missions during Operation Allied Force in April 1999. The front two aircraft are wearing the recently-adopted base codes. FA-121 wears the old style of serial presentation, and behind it, FA-91 wears the newer version with a revised fin flash. (KEY – Alan Warnes)

Right: Israeli F-16s were the first F-16s to be used in combat and have gained an impressive kill ratio, mostly against the Syrian Air Force over the Beka'a Valley during the occupation of Lebanon in 1982. Israeli F-16A and B models are referred to as *Netz* (Hawk) in Israeli service. F-16A 105 was one of the first four to arrive in Israel in July 1980, and is seen here in March 2000 with an enlarged Israeli Defence Force/Air Force (IDF/AF) roundel painted on the tail, standing on alert inside a Hardened Aircraft Shelter (HAS). (Shlomo Aloni)

Right: This 363rd TFW F-16C approaches a USAF KC-135 to top up its fuel tanks while performing a mission during Operation Desert Storm. It is carrying a pair of CBU-87 cluster bombs. (USAF)

Below: A pair of F-16s from the 510th FS, 31st FW, approach a USAF KC-135 Stratotanker while performing a mission during Operation Allied Force. (USAF – S/A Greg L Davis)

became President in 1999.) However, feelings within the air force were still high. During the second coup attempt, led by Brigadier General Visconti, the air force logistics service inspector, one Embraer AT-27 Tucano was shot down by an F-16, and a second F-16 was responsible for shooting down a pair of Rockwell OV-10 Broncos over Barquisimeto air base.

After the Gulf War ended, two no-fly zones were created above the 32nd Parallel over Northern Iraq as Operation Northern Watch and below the 36th Parallel in Southern Iraqi airspace as Operation Southern Watch. These no-fly zones were imposed largely to stop Saddam Hussein attacking the Kurds in the north and the Shi-ites in the south. During a Southern Watch mission on December 27, 1992, F-16D 90-0778 from the 33rd TFS/363rd TFW from Shaw AFB claimed an Iraqi AF MiG-25, one of a pair that had challenged several 4th TFW F-15E Strike Eagles. This was the first air-to-air kill by an American F-16 and was also the first official operational use of the AIM-120. On January 27, 1993, F-16C 86-0262 from the 23rd FS, deployed to Incirlik in Turkey as part of the 7440th Composite Wing (CW), shot down a MiG-29 while flying over Northern Iraq.

During peace-keeping operations over Bosnia, a two-ship formation of F-16Cs from the 526th FS 86 FW, based at Ramstein, shot down four out of a formation of six Serbian Air Force SOKO J-1 Jastrebs on February 28, 1994. The formation was spotted by an E-3 Sentry, bombing targets in the town of Bugojno. Two warnings, either to land or to leave the no-fly zone, were ignored and the two F-

Left: Photographed in April 1999 while flying an F-16D over the Adriatic Sea en route to the Former Republic of Yugoslavia (FRY) on an Operation Allied Force mission, a pilot from the 31st FW finds a moment to pose for the camera. (USAF – M/Sgt Keith Reed)

Left: The 31st FW Commander's aircraft launching down the runway at Aviano on April 21, 1999, carrying two LAU-68 rocket pods, two 2,000lb (907kg) iron bombs and four AIM-120 AMRAAMs. (USAF)

Below: During Operation Allied Force, Aviano, Italy, became one of the most crowded airfields in Europe. It usually houses the 31st FW, though as the tempo of the air campaign increased, the 31st was joined by F-16s from the 20th FW from Shaw AFB and the 52nd FW at Spangdahlem. This created something of a problem when it came to parking aircraft – shelters on the bases were already full and the other F-16s often had to be pushed into a space on the ramps around the HAS sites. (USAF – S/A Jeffery Allen)

16s were vectored on to them. The first aircraft, F-16C 89-2137, destroyed the leader with an AIM-120 and another two aircraft with a pair of AIM-9s, while the second F-16, 89-2009, claimed a fourth, again with an AIM-9.

Ten F-16Cs from the 555th Fighter Squadron from Aviano and four Dutch F-16s operating from Villafranca, both in Italy, were among the aircraft which took part in the NATO attack on the Republic of Serb Krajina airfield at Udbina on November 21, 1994. Dutch F-16A(R)s from 306 Squadron flew reconnaissance missions over Bosnia, and Turkish F-16Cs based at Ghedi, Italy, also participated, mainly flying Combat Air Patrols (CAPs). The F-16 AGM-88 HARM combination made its combat debut during Operation Deliberate Force, when an aircraft from the 23rd Fighter Squadron, operating from Spangdahlem AB, Germany, destroyed a Serbian radar site on September 8, 1995.

During Operation Allied Force in 1999, Belgian and Dutch aircraft operating from Amendola, Italy, performed both air-to-air and air-to-ground roles in Serbia and Kosovo. The air-to-air role was taken by Block 15 OCU aircraft and the air-to-ground missions by the F-16MLU aircraft. USAF F-16s operated mainly in the air-to-ground role, though they also undertook the secondary roles of Combat Search and Rescue (CSAR) and leaflet dropping. Danish, Norwegian, Portuguese and Turkish F-16s carried out CAPs over the Adriatic Sea and Bosnia Herzegovina. The Dutch AF scored a victory during the early hours of March 25, 1999, when F-16AM J-063 shot down a

Yugoslav MiG-29 using an AIM-120. On May 4, the USAF shot down a MiG-29 with an AIM-120 fired from F-16C 91-0353 of the 78th FS. The tally for the F-16 in air-to-air combat currently stands at 74 victories with no losses.

Top: Both the 20th and 52nd Fighter Wing operate Block 50 F-16Cs in the lethal SEAD roles. This aircraft from Spangdahlem departs Aviano carrying a standard load of two AIM-120 AMRAAMs, two AIM-9 Sidewinders and two AGM-88 HARMs, together with an AN/ALQ-131 ECM pod on the centreline pylon. (KEY – Steve Fletcher)

Above: With the Dolomites in the background, an F-16C Block 40 aircraft from the 31st FW returns to Aviano from a mission in March 1999. (KEY – Steve Fletcher)

Right Turkey participated in Operation Deny Flight over Bosnia, and regularly used USAF KC-135s for refuelling over the Adriatic Sea. (KEY – Duncan Cubitt)